Home for Dinner

Fresh Tastes, Quick Techniques, Easy Cooking

Lucy Waverman

RANDOM HOUSE CANADA

National Library of Canada Cataloguing in Publication Data

Waverman, Lucy
Home for dinner: fresh tastes, quick techniques, easy cooking / Lucy Waverman

ISBN: 0-679-31224-2

    1. Quick and easy cookery.   I. Title.

TX833.5.W378 2002   641.5'55   C2002-902184-7

Cover design: CS Richardson

Cover photography: Chris Freeland / Sautéed Halibut with Confit Spices

Food photography:
Colin Faulkner / Twice-Cooked Goat Cheese Soufflés, Roasted Spicy Salmon, Mexican Chicken, Chocolate Trifle
Rob Fiocca / Chilled Pea Soup with Mint
Per Kristiansen / Honey Garlic Spareribs
Vince Noguchi / Mushroom Risotto
David Scott / Zesty Beef and Mushroom Pie

Black and white photography:
Andreas Trauttmansdorff / pages vi, 8, 34, 56, 84, 106, 128, 150, 182
Natalie Kauffman / page 208

Interior design: Sharon Foster Design
Typesetting: Janine Laporte

Printed and bound in Canada

10 9 8 7 6 5 4 3 2 1

Contents

Introduction

Home for Dinner features recipes for the 21st century — dishes with interesting themes, perfect for relaxed entertaining or family dinners. The recipes are easy, yet each one has a flavor twist that takes it out of the ordinary.

I want people to feel comfortable in the kitchen and to have success when they make my recipes — so they will want to keep cooking. Cooking is knowledge-based. The more you know about a recipe, its ingredients and cooking methods, the more accomplished a cook you will become. The boxed tips and chapter on today's store cupboard are aimed at making cooking at home even easier and more convenient.

This book features a new chapter, "Slow and Fast." The slow food movement began as a reaction to the fast foods of the McDonald's era. The movement embodied a desire to return to the comfort foods of an earlier time, when evening meals were carefully prepared by traditional methods, using local, seasonal ingredients; the results were then enjoyed over a long, social dinner. Although it was the Italians who first revived this artisan approach to cooking, the trend has spread across the ocean. We now have slow food organizations in both Canada and the United States.

But slow food is only a small part of this book. Other chapters feature elegant soups, quick appetizers and main courses that sizzle with taste. Fish, an increasingly enticing main course, fits the ideal of healthy, fast and flavorful food. Look for recipes that feature popular fish, as well as some that highlight less well known varieties such as skate. Noodles are no longer just pasta — and my recipes encompass a world of international flavours from Asia through to Australia. My desserts are always simple, some fruity, others easy no-fail baking.

Home entertaining is becoming popular again as people retrench and seek familiarity in a world that is in a state of flux. And more and more of us are realizing that good times center around family, good friends, good conversation and great food.

I hope **Home for Dinner** will help to bring good times to your dinner table, too.

Lucy Waverman

CHAPTER 1

The Store Cupboard

If you can organize your kitchen, you can organize your life.
– Louis Parrish

The Store Cupboard

A well-stocked store cupboard means you will have on hand the basic ingredients and seasonings for everyday cooking, including most of the ingredients that you will need to make the recipes in this book.

My store cupboard is a reflection of how we eat at my home. Yours should reflect your own style.

Some items should be transferred to the refrigerator or freezer (e.g., coconut milk) once they have been opened; check the labels.

Seasonings and Condiments
Dijon mustard (grainy and smooth)
ketchup
hot pepper sauce
Worcestershire sauce
sea salt
kosher salt (a coarse, additive-free salt with large flakes that dissolve easily)
black peppercorns (ground pepper loses its potency almost immediately, so use whole peppercorns and a pepper mill)
dry mustard
good-quality chicken and beef bouillon cubes (make sure chicken or beef appears near the top of the ingredients list)

Oils and Vinegars
vegetable oil
olive oil (a regular olive oil for cooking, a mid-range extra-virgin oil for salad dressings, and a good extra-virgin oil for drizzling on soups and pizzas)
red and white wine vinegar
sherry vinegar
white vinegar
balsamic vinegar (an inexpensive balsamic vinegar for cooking and an aged one for sprinkling on vegetables and poultry before serving)

Pasta, Rice, Grains and Beans
long-grain rice
risotto rice (e.g., Arborio or Carnaroli)
brown rice
dried pasta in various long and short shapes
cornmeal
barley
Israeli couscous
Moroccan couscous
bulgur
buckwheat
lentils
dried beans (such as red and white kidney beans and black beans; beans keep for years if stored in an airtight container)

Canned Goods

salmon

tuna

jams and jellies

peanut butter

low-sodium chicken and beef broth

plum tomatoes (look for San Marzano or organic plum tomatoes)

tomato paste

tomato sauce

roasted red peppers

capers

salsa

pesto

hot pickled peppers

horseradish

mayonnaise

tapenade

marinated artichokes

beans (kidney beans, white beans, chickpeas, lentils, black beans)

Dried Goods

sun-dried tomatoes

dried mushrooms (shiitake, porcini)

dried fruits (raisins, cranberries, apricots)

coconut

herbs and spices, such as basil, tarragon, rosemary, oregano, fennel, cumin, paprika, coriander seeds, ground ginger, cayenne, cinnamon, hot red pepper flakes, chili powder, bay leaves, saffron (buy whole spices and grind as you need them with a coffee grinder or spice grinder; buy dried herb leaves instead of powdered herbs)

Asian Ingredients

soy sauce

Asian chili sauce

hoisin sauce

oyster sauce

dried Chinese mushrooms

curry paste (Indian and Thai green and red)

miso

sesame oil

rice vinegar (seasoned and regular)

rice noodles

rice paper wrappers

wasabi powder

coconut milk

Asian rices (short-grain Japanese sushi rice, Thai jasmine rice, basmati rice, sticky rice)

Baking Ingredients

baking powder

baking soda

all-purpose flour

whole wheat flour

bran

rolled oats

cornstarch

vanilla extract

almond extract

sugar (icing sugar, brown sugar, granulated sugar)

cocoa

molasses

chocolate (unsweetened, bittersweet, semisweet, white)

corn syrup

honey

In the Refrigerator

The refrigerator is also an important part of your store cupboard. Mine always contains olives, anchovies, eggs, cheeses (e.g., Cheddar, Parmesan and cream cheese), sour cream, yogurt, milk and unsalted butter. I keep all nuts in the freezer (to prevent them from going rancid), along with fresh and dry breadcrumbs. Clean out your refrigerator often, and always check Best Before dates.

GARLIC AND GINGER

Fresh ginger root and garlic should be stored loose in a cupboard or on the counter. If refrigerated, they will deteriorate quickly.

FRESH VS. DRIED HERBS

While most of the recipes in this book call for fresh herbs, you can usually substitute dried. As dried herbs are much more potent than fresh, use one-third as much (e.g., 1 tbsp chopped fresh herb equals 1 tsp dried).

STORE CUPBOARD RECIPES

Here are some basic spice mixtures, oils and vinegars that can be kept on hand to make cooking even easier.

BARBECUE RUB

Sprinkle liberally on steaks or chops before barbecuing.

 2 tbsp paprika
 2 tbsp chili powder
 2 tsp dry mustard
 2 tsp dried thyme
 2 tsp kosher salt
 1 1/2 tsp freshly ground pepper

Combine all ingredients and keep in container in cupboard.

 Makes about 1/2 cup.

JERK RUB

Sprinkle on steaks, chicken and pork to add an authentic Caribbean flavor.

 1/2 tsp dried thyme
 1 tsp ground allspice
 2 tsp granulated sugar
 1/2 tsp ground nutmeg
 1/2 tsp cinnamon
 1 tsp hot red pepper flakes
 1 tsp freshly ground pepper

Combine all ingredients and keep in container in cupboard.

 Makes about 2 tbsp.

CRACKED PEPPER RUB

Sprinkle on meat, chicken or fish for a subtle peppery taste.

2 tbsp cumin seeds
2 tbsp coriander seeds
1 tsp fennel seeds
2 tbsp black peppercorns

Place all ingredients in skillet on medium heat and cook until fragrant. Cool. Transfer to plastic bag and bash with pot until coarsely ground. Keep in container in cupboard.

Makes about 1/3 cup.

GARAM MASALA

Garam translates into "hot spices," meaning that the spices raise your body heat, but the mixture is more fragrant than hot. It can be used like a curry powder but is often added at the end of cooking to highlight flavors. You can buy garam masala, but making your own will give a much fresher taste to everything you use it in.

2 tbsp cardamom seeds
2 3-inch cinnamon sticks
1 tbsp whole cloves
3 tbsp black peppercorns
1/2 cup cumin seeds
1/2 cup coriander seeds

Place all spices in dry skillet over medium heat. Cook, stirring frequently, until spices darken slightly and smell fragrant, about 2 to 4 minutes. Remove from heat immediately.

Grind spices until powdery. Cool and store in an airtight jar for up to 6 months.

Makes about 1 1/4 cups.

HERBES DE PROVENCE

Use this herb mixture to enhance Mediterranean dishes, stews, roast chicken and pizza. If you can find them, dried lavender flowers add a wonderful bouquet.

2 tbsp dried thyme
2 tbsp dried savory
2 tbsp dried marjoram
2 tbsp dried rosemary
1 tbsp dried lavender
1 tbsp cracked fennel seeds
1 tbsp cracked coriander seeds
2 bay leaves, broken in pieces

Combine all herbs and spices. Store in airtight container for up to 1 year.

Makes about 1 cup.

ASIAN VINEGAR

A citrus-scented, fragrant vinegar with a punch. Use for Thai or Vietnamese cooking, especially noodle soups and salads. Keeps indefinitely.

  1 stalk lemon grass
  4 thin slices ginger
  2 Kaffir lime leaves or 1-inch piece lime rind
  2 Thai chilies, cut in half, or 1 tbsp Asian chili paste
  3 cups rice vinegar or cider vinegar

Remove outer leaves of lemon grass and cut off green top. Finely chop remaining tender white bulb (about 2 inches).

Place lemon grass, ginger, lime leaves, chilies and vinegar in pot. Bring to simmer, then set aside to cool.

Strain and return vinegar to bottle. Add fresh chilies and a fresh lemon grass stalk to strained vinegar for decoration if you wish.

Makes 3 cups.

GINGER CHILI OIL

Use this spicy oil sparingly in stir-fries or to liven up a soup or salsa. Store in a cool place but do not refrigerate. It will keep for one month.

  ¼ cup sliced ginger
  3 tbsp hot red pepper flakes
  2 cups vegetable oil

Combine ginger, hot pepper flakes and oil in pot. Bring to simmer and simmer over low heat for 10 minutes. Remove from heat, strain and cool.

Makes about 2 cups.

GREEN HERB OIL

This will keep, refrigerated, for three months. Make sure herbs are always covered with oil.

  1 cup coarsely chopped mixed herbs (e.g., parsley, coriander, basil and mint)
  2 cups vegetable oil or olive oil

Add herbs to oil in pot. Bring to simmer and simmer for 10 minutes. Remove from heat and cool. Let sit overnight, then strain into bottle.

Makes about 2 cups.

HARISSA

The heat of the sauce is dependent on the heat of the chilies. If you want this hotter, add cayenne to taste. Use as a condiment for Moroccan dishes. It will keep, refrigerated, for up to one month.

  6 dried chili peppers, such as ancho or New Mexican
  2 tsp dried mint leaves
  4 cloves garlic
  2 tsp coriander seeds
  2 tsp caraway seeds
  1 tsp cumin seeds
  2 tbsp olive oil

Quarter, seed and stem chilies. Soak chilies and mint in hot water for 30 minutes or until softened. Drain through sieve.

Add garlic cloves and spices through feed tube of food processor with machine running. Add chilies, mint and olive oil. Puree until smooth.

Makes about ¾ cup.

CHAPTER 2

Appetizers and Soups

My idea of heaven is eating pâté de foie gras to the sound of trumpets.
— Sydney Smith

CARAMELIZED ONIONS ON SWEET POTATO SCONES

This tasty scone is wonderful with the caramelized onions, but you could also top with tapenade or salsa for a quick and easy appetizer. These scones reheat well.

SWEET POTATO SCONES

1 large sweet potato (about 1 lb)

1 tbsp olive oil

Salt and freshly ground pepper to taste

1 cup all-purpose flour

1/2 tsp chopped fresh rosemary or pinch dried

1 tbsp butter, melted

· · · · ·

CARAMELIZED ONIONS

1 tbsp olive oil

2 tbsp butter

6 cups sliced Spanish or sweet onions

1 tbsp granulated sugar

Salt and freshly ground pepper to taste

2 tbsp sherry vinegar

1/2 cup chicken stock

1/2 cup whipping cream

20 fresh sage leaves, slivered

Preheat oven to 400 F.

Brush sweet potato with oil, salt and pepper. Prick potato and roast for 40 to 45 minutes or until soft. Cool, peel and mash.

Measure out 1 cup sweet potato and combine with flour, rosemary and butter to form soft dough.

Roll dough out on floured board until 1/4 inch thick. Cut out scones with 2-inch round cutter. Re-roll leftover pastry.

Cook scones in batches in oiled non-stick skillet over low heat for about 2 minutes per side or until flecked with brown and cooked in the middle. Drain on paper towels.

Prepare onions while sweet potato is roasting. Heat oil and butter in large skillet on medium heat until butter sizzles. Add onions and sauté for 3 minutes or until onions start to soften.

Sprinkle in sugar, salt and pepper. Reduce heat to medium-low and continue to cook, stirring occasionally, until onions turn golden brown, about 20 minutes.

Stir in vinegar, stock and whipping cream. Increase heat to medium-high and reduce until onions become a thick mass, about 4 minutes. Stir in sage. Taste and adjust seasonings if necessary.

Top scones with caramelized onions. Serve hot or at room temperature.

ASPARAGUS, GOAT CHEESE AND WALNUT TART

SERVES 4

This goat cheese pastry can be used for any savory pie or flan, but it goes beautifully with this filling. It is easy to make and can be rolled out or patted into the pan.

You can make this as individual tarts or as a single large tart. The pastry can also be cut into rounds and baked to serve as a savory cookie.

PASTRY	FILLING
1 cup all-purpose flour	16 stalks asparagus, trimmed
1/3 cup crumbled goat cheese	2 eggs, beaten
1/3 cup butter, diced	1/2 cup whipping cream
1/2 tsp salt	1/4 cup crumbled goat cheese
Freshly ground pepper to taste	Salt and freshly ground pepper to taste
· · · · ·	1/4 cup chopped walnuts

Place flour in food processor. Add cheese, butter, salt and pepper. Pulse machine until mixture resembles small peas. Remove from processor and form into ball. Wrap in plastic wrap and chill for 30 minutes.

Preheat oven to 400 F.

Peel asparagus stalks if thick. Bring large skillet of water to boil. Add asparagus and simmer for 2 minutes or until crisp-tender. Immediately drain and run under cold water until cool. Reserve tips for garnish and cut stalks into 3-inch pieces.

Pat or roll out pastry to fit 8-inch tart pan. Line pastry with parchment paper or foil. Place dried beans or pie weights in pastry and bake for 10 minutes. Remove weights and paper. Prick pastry and bake for 5 minutes or until pale gold. Reduce oven temperature to 350 F.

Combine eggs, cream and cheese. Season well with salt and pepper. Stir in asparagus stalks.

Pour cream mixture into pastry shell. Garnish with asparagus tips. Sprinkle walnuts over tart.

Bake for 20 to 25 minutes or until custard is set.

ICED CAMEMBERT WITH WARM SESAME CRACKERS

SERVES 8 TO 10

Serving the mixture icy cold with the warm crackers makes a great but simple hors d'oeuvre. Make the crackers yourself or buy them and heat at 350 F for 3 to 5 minutes before serving.

1 lb ripe Camembert or Brie

Pinch paprika

Pinch cayenne

Freshly ground pepper to taste

½ cup whipping cream

Watercress for garnish

30 sesame crackers, warm

· · · · ·

Remove rind from Camembert and dice the cheese. In food processor or by hand, combine cheese, paprika, cayenne, pepper and ¼ cup whipping cream.

Whisk remaining ¼ cup cream until thick and fold into cheese mixture.

Line small ring mold or loaf pan with plastic wrap. Spoon in cheese mixture and chill overnight.

Turn out cheese onto serving plate and garnish with watercress. Serve with warm sesame crackers.

SESAME CRACKERS

Combine 1 cup all-purpose flour, 1 tbsp black sesame seeds, ½ tsp baking powder and 1 tsp salt. Cut in ¼ cup butter until mixture resembles coarse breadcrumbs. Slowly blend in ¼ cup cold water to make soft dough.

Roll out dough on floured board until ⅛ inch thick. Prick with fork and cut into 2-inch rounds. Place on lightly oiled or parchment paper–lined baking sheet.

Bake at 375 F for 10 to 12 minutes or until crisp and golden.

Makes about 30 crackers.

SUSHI RICE APPETIZER

SERVES 6

Not entirely authentic, but a fun way to make and serve sushi. Guests make their own rolls using nori, rice and garnishes of their choice. Serve bowls of wasabi and soy sauce alongside for dipping.

Use Japanese short-grain rice in this recipe if you can. Buy seasoned rice vinegar or make your own.

2 cups short-grain Japanese rice
2¼ cups cold water
½ cup seasoned rice vinegar
6 sheets nori, cut in quarters

Sushi garnishes, such as sliced avocado, cucumber sticks, green onions, crabmeat, smoked or raw salmon, salmon caviar, thinly sliced seared tuna, grilled shrimp and pickled ginger

Place rice in colander and rinse with cold water until water runs clear. Drain rice very well.

Place rice in heavy pot and cover with cold water. Bring to boil, cover immediately, reduce heat to low and steam for 15 to 20 minutes or until rice is cooked.

Transfer rice to a large, shallow bowl and cool for 10 minutes.

Pour vinegar slowly over cooked rice and combine gently. Cool, then cover with damp cloth until ready to serve.

Mound rice on large platter and surround with nori and garnishes. Let guests assemble their own rolls by forming piece of nori into cone and filling with rice and garnishes.

SEASONED VINEGAR

Combine ½ cup rice vinegar, 2 tbsp granulated sugar and ¾ tsp salt in pot on low heat. Stir until sugar dissolves. Cool. Stir together just before pouring over rice.

Makes about ½ cup.

TWICE-COOKED GOAT CHEESE SOUFFLÉS

SERVES 6

This is an impressive first course that's stress-free, since the soufflés are cooked ahead of time and then reheated. They puff up again when they are rebaked. Surround with a mesclun salad dressed with a mustardy vinaigrette.

½ cup grated Parmesan cheese	1 tbsp Dijon mustard
5 tbsp butter	8 oz goat cheese, crumbled
5 tbsp all-purpose flour	6 eggs, separated
2 cups warm milk	Salt and freshly ground pepper to taste
1 tbsp chopped fresh thyme or 1 tsp dried	1 cup whipping cream

Preheat oven to 375 F.

Oil six 1-cup soufflé dishes and dust with Parmesan. Reserve remaining Parmesan.

Heat butter in pot on medium heat and slowly stir in flour. Cook for 2 minutes, stirring. Slowly stir in warm milk and thyme. Bring to boil, stirring. Stir in mustard and half the goat cheese until combined. Cool slightly.

Beat egg yolks and whisk into milk base. Season with salt and pepper.

Whisk egg whites in large bowl until they hold soft peaks. Stir one-quarter of egg whites into milk-yolk mixture to lighten it. Fold in remaining whites and goat cheese.

Fill soufflé dishes. Place dishes in roasting pan and fill roasting pan with hot water until it comes halfway up sides of soufflé dishes.

Bake for 15 minutes or until well risen and golden.

Remove soufflés from oven and let sit on rack for 10 minutes. Loosen sides of soufflés with knife. Turn soufflés out into shallow baking dish. Cover loosely and refrigerate for up to one day. Return to room temperature before baking.Preheat oven to 400 F.

Pour cream over and around soufflés in baking dish. Sprinkle tops with remaining Parmesan.

Bake for 12 to 15 minutes or until puffed and golden. Serve immediately.

ROASTED GARLIC AND LIMA BEAN CROSTINI

SERVES 4

This combination may sound strange, but it tastes terrific. The dip is a pretty green color and a cinch to make. It can also be served in a bowl and surrounded with root vegetable chips for dipping. This may also be made with fava beans.

2 heads roasted garlic (page 78)	2 tsp lime juice or to taste
1 cup frozen lima beans, defrosted	Salt and freshly ground pepper to taste
2/3 cup olive oil	Pinch cayenne
1/4 cup grated Parmesan cheese	12 thin slices Italian bread
1/4 cup chopped fresh mint	. . . . .

Squeeze garlic out of heads and place in food processor. Add beans and 1/2 cup olive oil. Process until smooth.

Stir in Parmesan, mint, lime juice, salt, pepper and cayenne.

Brush bread on both sides with remaining 2 tbsp olive oil and grill on each side until golden. Top with bean mixture.

PREPARING FAVA BEANS

Split open pods and remove beans. Blanch beans in boiling water for 30 seconds. Drain and immediately stir into ice water to cool.

Slip tough outer skins from beans and discard. The beans are ready for eating either raw or lightly cooked.

1 lb fava beans in the pod = 1 cup shelled beans

1 cup shelled beans = 1/2 cup skinned beans

FAVA BEAN DIP WITH PESTO

In food processor, puree 1 cup cooked fava beans with 1/2 tsp chopped garlic and 1/4 cup mayonnaise. Stir in 1/4 cup chopped chives and lemon juice to taste. Place in bowl and streak with 1 tbsp pesto (page 60).

Makes about 1 cup.

PARMESAN CUPS WITH MUSHROOM PERSILLADE

SERVES 4

Parmesan cups can be used as a base for any kind of filling. You can also leave flat and use as a garnish for salads. Store them in an airtight tin; do not refrigerate or they will become soggy.

¹/₂ cup coarsely grated Parmesan cheese	3 tbsp butter
¹/₄ cup chopped parsley	1¹/₂ lb mixed mushrooms, trimmed and quartered
1 tbsp chopped garlic	Salt and freshly ground pepper to taste
2 tsp grated lemon rind	4 cups red oak leaf or other lettuce
5 tbsp olive oil	2 tbsp balsamic vinegar

Preheat oven to 350 F.

Place 2 tbsp Parmesan on parchment-lined baking sheet. Shape into lacy 4-inch circle. Repeat with remaining Parmesan to make 4 circles.

Bake rounds for 5 minutes or until pale gold. Mold onto backs of small bowls, muffin cups or glasses. Let cool and unmold.

Combine parsley, garlic and lemon rind.

Heat 3 tbsp oil and butter in skillet over high heat. Add mushrooms and sauté until golden and juices have disappeared, about 4 to 5 minutes. Stir in parsley mixture. Cook for 1 minute. Season well with salt and pepper.

Place Parmesan cups on individual serving plates. Surround with lettuce. Fill cups with mushroom mixture, letting mixture spill over onto lettuce.

Return skillet to low heat. Whisk balsamic vinegar and remaining 2 tbsp olive oil into any pan juices. Pour dressing over lettuce and mushrooms.

BAKED RICOTTA WITH PESTO

SERVES 8

My former recipe tester Penny Higgins came back from a trip to Australia raving about the many baked ricotta recipes that were all the rage there. They are excellent and easy to pre-pare. Serve with sliced tomatoes and onions drizzled with extra-virgin olive oil as a first course or side dish.

3 eggs	¼ cup pesto (page 60)
2 cups ricotta	¾ cup grilled peppers, cut in thin strips
1 cup grated Parmesan cheese	1 tsp paprika
Salt and freshly ground pepper to taste	1 tbsp olive oil

Preheat oven to 350 F. Oil loaf pan and line base with parchment paper or waxed paper.

Beat eggs. Stir in ricotta and Parmesan and beat together until well mixed. Season with salt and pepper.

Pour half the mixture into loaf pan. Cover with pesto and peppers. Pour remaining cheese mixture on top.

Sprinkle with paprika and pour over oil.

Bake for 1 hour or until puffed and golden. Cool.

Turn out loaf onto plate. Remove paper and flip over onto serving plate so golden side is up.

GRILLED PEPPERS

Cut peppers in half. Grill skin side down on bar-becue until skin is blackened, about 5 minutes. (If using broiler, grill skin side up.)

Cool peppers and slip off skins. Cut peppers into strips.

SPINACH AND GARLIC SCAPE PESTO

MAKES ABOUT 2 CUPS

This pesto can be tossed with cooked pasta (add a little pasta water to thin out the sauce). You can also pile the pesto on baked potatoes or use as a topping for crostini or as a garnish for soups.

If scapes are not available use 1/2 cup garlic chives and 1 tbsp chopped garlic.

2 cups baby spinach	1/4 cup olive oil
1/2 cup chopped garlic scapes	2 tbsp butter, at room temperature
1/4 cup grated Parmesan cheese	Salt and freshly ground pepper to taste

Place spinach, scapes and Parmesan cheese in food processor. Pulse until mixture is chunky. With machine running, pour olive oil down feed tube.

Add butter, salt and pepper and process until smooth.

GARLIC SCAPES

Scapes are the edible curly tops and seed pods of hard-necked garlic, which form in the early summer. The tops must be trimmed from the plants to allow the garlic cloves to mature properly. The taste of the scapes is much milder than the garlic cloves. In Mediterranean countries scapes are often served as a vegetable or tossed with pasta.

VEGETABLE CHEESE STRUDEL

SERVES 4 to 6

One of my favorite vegetarian dishes, this also makes a fine main course. Vary the vegetables (try using Asian eggplant or asparagus). If smoked cheese is not available, or if you don't care for it, use Fontina or Cheddar.

2 tbsp olive oil	6 shiitake mushrooms, trimmed and sliced
1/2 red pepper, thinly sliced	1 tbsp chopped fresh mint
1 tsp chopped garlic	1 1/2 cups grated smoked Gruyère cheese
1 tsp chopped ginger	Salt and freshly ground pepper to taste
2 leeks, trimmed and chopped	1 package frozen puff pastry, defrosted
1 small zucchini, thinly sliced	1 egg, beaten, with a pinch of salt
1 cup thinly sliced fennel	• • • • •

Preheat oven to 400 F.

Heat olive oil in skillet on medium-high heat. Add red pepper and sauté for 2 minutes. Add garlic, ginger, leeks, zucchini, fennel and mushrooms. Sauté until crisp-tender, about 2 minutes. Stir in mint and cheese. Season with salt and pepper and cool.

Roll out half of pastry to a 14 x 10-inch rectangle (reserve remaining pastry for another use). Pile vegetables lengthwise along upper third of pastry, leaving 1-inch border on short sides. Brush all outside borders with beaten egg. Fold short ends up over filling, then roll into cylinder. Place seam side down on baking sheet and prick top. Brush with egg.

Bake for 20 to 25 minutes or until golden brown.

TOMATO VINAIGRETTE

Combine 3 chopped tomatoes, 2 tbsp red wine vinegar, 1 tsp chopped jalapeño pepper and 1 tsp coriander seeds in food processor. Puree until smooth. Pour 1/4 cup olive oil down feed tube with machine running. Stir in 2 tbsp chopped fresh coriander and season with salt and pepper to taste.

Makes about 1 cup.

Slice strudel and drizzle with vinaigrette.

ZUCCHINI DIP

SERVES 6

Serve this dip with warm pappadums or grilled tortillas cut in quarters.

1 tbsp vegetable oil	½ cup coconut milk
2 zucchini, chopped	¼ cup mayonnaise
1 tsp grated ginger	1 tbsp lime juice
1 tsp Thai green curry paste	2 tbsp chopped fresh coriander

Heat oil in skillet on medium heat. Add zucchini, ginger and curry paste. Sauté until zucchini softens slightly, about 2 minutes. Add coconut milk. Bring to boil, reduce heat, cover and simmer for 10 minutes or until zucchini is soft.

Puree contents of skillet in food processor until smooth. Stir in mayonnaise, lime juice and coriander.

CURRY PASTES

Thai curry pastes and Indian curry pastes are entirely different. Both can be found at supermarkets and Asian grocery stores. Red Thai curry paste is made with red chilies and is milder than green curry paste, which is made with green chilies and is very spicy.

Indian curry pastes are made by cooking Indian curry spices in oil. Various types such as Madras or Vindaloo are interchangeable, but the heats are different. I use a medium blend.

CURRIED APPLE AND AVOCADO SOUP

SERVES 4

A mysterious, summery, cold soup. You can use Indian curry paste, but the taste will not be as exotic. If the soup becomes too thick, thin with extra stock. Taste for seasoning after refrigeration as cold subdues flavours.

2 tbsp butter	3 cups chicken stock
1 small onion, chopped	1 avocado, peeled and chopped
1 tsp grated ginger	1/2 cup whipping cream
1 tsp green Thai curry paste	Salt and freshly ground pepper to taste
1 green apple, peeled and chopped	2 tbsp chopped chives
1 tsp granulated sugar	· · · · ·

Heat butter in pot on medium heat. Sauté onion until soft but not brown, about 2 minutes. Stir in ginger, curry paste and apple and cook for 1 minute.

Add sugar and stock. Bring to boil, reduce heat and simmer for 10 minutes or until apple is tender.

Puree soup in food processor or with hand blender. Add avocado and puree again.

Pour mixture into bowl. Stir in cream, salt and pepper. Refrigerate (this soup should be served very cold). Serve garnished with chopped chives.

HAND IMMERSION BLENDERS

Chefs often use these inexpensive hand tools to blend soups and sauces without any fuss. They give soups a smoother texture than a food processor. Afterwards you just rinse them and hang them up.

JERUSALEM ARTICHOKE SOUP

SERVES 4

Jerusalem artichokes are not artichokes, although they have a slight artichoke flavor. They are knobby tubers that look a bit like ginger root. Sauté them in butter (page 181), roast with olive oil and herbs or make this fine soup.

1 lb Jerusalem artichokes	¼ cup whipping cream
2 tbsp butter	Salt and freshly ground pepper to taste
1 cup chopped onions	2 tbsp chopped mint
1 tsp grated ginger	1 tbsp lime juice
4 cups chicken stock	• • • • •

Peel or scrape artichokes with knife and cut into large dice.

Heat butter in pot on medium heat. Add onions and ginger and sauté until softened, about 3 minutes. Add artichokes and sauté for another 2 minutes.

Add stock and bring to boil. Reduce heat and simmer for 15 minutes or until artichokes are tender.

Puree soup in food processor or with hand blender. Return to pot, add cream and stir in salt, pepper, mint and lime juice.

CHICKEN STOCK

If you don't have time to make homemade stock, buy chicken broth in Tetrapak containers or purchase stock from the butcher. You can always improve packaged or canned stock by simmering it with some cut-up carrots, onions and several chicken wings. Commercial stocks are often very salty; if you use them, dilute with twice the amount of water called for.

CURRIED CARROT BISQUE

SERVES 6

Carrot soup can be a bit bland without an injection of flavor; in this soup, curry powder provides the added zing.

2 tbsp butter	1 tsp chopped garlic
1 lb carrots, peeled and sliced	1 tsp curry powder
1 cup chopped onions	5 cups chicken stock
1 cup peeled, diced potatoes	1/2 cup whipping cream
1 tsp dried ground ginger	Salt and freshly ground pepper to taste

Heat butter in heavy pot over medium heat. Stir in carrots, onions and potatoes. Sauté for about 5 minutes or until onions soften.

Add ginger, garlic and curry powder. Sauté for 2 minutes.

Pour in chicken stock and bring to boil. Reduce heat and simmer for 20 to 25 minutes or until vegetables are tender.

Puree with hand blender or in food processor. Return to heat, add whipping cream, salt and pepper. Simmer for 5 minutes.

CURRIED CREAM OF CELERY ROOT SOUP

Celery root may look ugly and gnarled, but its herbaceous celery-parsley taste makes it a winner in salads and soups. Substitute celery root for the carrots in the above recipe for a different take. The celery root will take about 5 minutes less time to cook.

CHICKEN SOUP WITH DILL AND EGGS

SERVES 4

A Greek version of chicken soup that uses Israeli couscous instead of the traditional rice. It is best made using homemade stock.

6 cups chicken stock

1/2 cup Israeli couscous

2 eggs, beaten

2 tbsp lemon juice

2 tbsp chopped fresh dill

Salt and freshly ground pepper to taste

Bring stock to boil in large pot on high heat. Slowly stir in couscous. Reduce heat and simmer for 10 minutes or until couscous is softened.

Beat together eggs, lemon juice and dill. Slowly stir in several ladlefuls of soup. Return warm egg mixture to soup and cook together for 2 to 3 minutes. (Do not boil or soup will curdle.) Season well with salt and pepper.

ISRAELI COUSCOUS

Israeli couscous looks like pearl barley, but it is actually a tiny round pasta (also known as pearl pasta) that has been toasted. It is not related to Moroccan couscous. Israeli couscous is slightly chewy and buttery-tasting; it is often served as a side dish or salad.

CORN CHOWDER WITH CHIPOTLE PEPPERS

SERVES 4

The smokiness and spice of this lovely soup can be enhanced with 2 oz smoked bacon. Chop the bacon and sauté with the onions.

2 tbsp olive oil	1/3 cup diced green pepper
3/4 cup chopped onions	4 1/2 cups chicken stock
1 tbsp chopped garlic	1 bay leaf
3 cups fresh corn kernels, reserving cobs	1 tsp finely chopped chipotle pepper
1/3 cup diced red pepper	2 tbsp chopped fresh coriander

Heat 2 tbsp olive oil in pot on medium heat. Add onions, garlic, corn kernels and red and green peppers. Sauté for about 5 minutes, mixing well.

Add stock, reserved corn cobs, bay leaf and chipotle and bring to boil. Reduce heat and simmer for about 10 minutes or until corn is tender. Remove and discard corn cobs and bay leaf.

Puree all but **1/2** cup corn mixture in food processor or using hand blender.

Return pureed soup to pot and add reserved corn mixture. Cook for 5 minutes. Sprinkle with coriander.

FRESH CORN KERNELS

To remove corn kernels from the cob, slice down between the rows with a knife. Using the back of the knife, scrape off the kernels and their milky liquid into a bowl. One large corn cob should yield about 1 cup kernels.

CHIPOTLE PEPPERS

High on the chili heat scale, chipotle peppers are smoked jalapeños that have been preserved in a tomato sauce. Look for cans of chipotle in adobo, which can be found at upscale grocery stores or any Mexican or South American store. Although there is no substitute for their smokiness, you could use Asian chili sauce instead.

SEAFOOD LAKSA

SERVES 4

I devoured this hearty soup when I visited Australia. Its Malaysian culinary roots feature an interesting mix of Thai and Indian flavors. Serve in larger quantities as a light supper dish.

8 oz broad rice noodles	Grated rind of 2 limes
2 stalks lemon grass	16 mussels
1 2-inch piece ginger, peeled	12 scallops
1 onion, peeled and quartered	4 oz squid rings
2 tbsp vegetable oil	2 tbsp lime juice
2 tbsp Indian curry paste	Salt and freshly ground pepper to taste
1 tsp granulated sugar	2 tbsp chopped fresh coriander
1 14-oz (398 mL) can coconut milk	¼ cup thinly sliced green onions
4 cups chicken stock or fish stock	1 red chili, thinly sliced, optional
2 tbsp Thai fish sauce	• • • • •

Soak rice noodles in hot water for 30 minutes or until softened.

Cut off top section of lemon grass and discard. Remove tough outer leaves. Coarsely chop tender bulb and add to food processor with ginger and onion. Process until finely chopped.

Heat oil in large pot on medium heat. Add onion mixture and sauté until fragrant, about 2 minutes. Add curry paste and sugar and sauté for 30 seconds.

Add coconut milk, stock, fish sauce and lime rind and bring to boil. Reduce heat and simmer for 20 minutes.

Add mussels and scallops and simmer for 3 minutes. Add squid and cook for 2 minutes or until mussels open and scallops are opaque. Add lime juice. Season with salt and pepper. Taste and adjust seasonings, adding more lime juice or fish sauce to taste.

Bring large pot of water to boil and add noodles. Blanch for 1 minute, then drain. Divide noodles among 4 large bowls.

Ladle soup and seafood over noodles. Garnish with coriander, green onions and sliced chili.

ROASTED GARLIC AND LEEK SOUP

SERVES 4

A flavorful soup that contains practically no fat.

2 heads garlic	1 tbsp olive oil
4 cups chicken stock	2 tsp chopped fresh thyme or $1/2$ tsp dried
2 leeks, trimmed and halved	Salt and freshly ground pepper to taste
1 white turnip, peeled and sliced	2 tbsp finely chopped parsley

Preheat oven to 450 F.

Separate garlic cloves and remove papery outer skin. Cut off root end. Bring stock to boil in pot and blanch garlic for 2 minutes.

Remove garlic from stock and slide cloves out of skins. Reserve stock and garlic separately.

Brush garlic cloves, leeks and turnip with olive oil. Roast for 8 minutes or until browned. Slice leeks thickly.

Combine vegetables in pot with stock and thyme. Bring to boil, reduce heat and simmer for 10 minutes or until vegetables are softened.

Puree soup in food processor or with hand blender. Return to pot, add salt and pepper and reheat. Garnish with parsley.

LEMON GRASS SQUASH SOUP WITH TOASTED COCONUT

SERVES 6

The combination of fragrant flavors make this soup an outstanding first course. Garnish with the coconut or with grated deep-fried squash.

2 tbsp vegetable oil

2 cups chopped onions

2 tbsp chopped lemon grass

1 tbsp grated lime rind

5 cups peeled and cubed butternut squash

5 cups chicken stock

Salt and freshly ground pepper to taste

1/2 cup whipping cream

1/3 cup toasted, grated unsweetened coconut

· · · · ·

Heat oil in pot on medium heat. Add onions, lemon grass and lime rind. Sauté for 2 minutes or until onions begin to soften. Add squash and sauté for 2 minutes.

Pour in chicken stock and bring to boil. Reduce heat and simmer for 20 minutes or until squash is cooked.

Blend in food processor or with hand blender. Season well with salt and pepper. Return to pot and add cream. Bring to boil, reduce heat and simmer for 2 minutes.

Serve soup garnished with toasted coconut.

TOASTING COCONUT

Spread grated unsweetened coconut on baking sheet. Bake in preheated 350 F oven for 10 minutes or until golden.

LEMON SPINACH BOUILLABAISSE

SERVES 4

Saffron gives this soup an unusual look and Mediterranean flavor, but you can omit it if you can't find it.

2 tbsp olive oil	2 tsp grated lemon rind
1 tsp chopped garlic	Salt and freshly ground pepper to taste
1 cup chopped onions	• • • • •
1 cup peeled, chopped Yukon Gold potatoes	GARNISH
6 cups sliced spinach	1/4 cup sour cream
4 cups chicken stock	1 tsp lemon juice
1/2 tsp saffron threads	1 tsp grated lemon rind
1/2 tsp dried thyme	2 tsp finely chopped parsley
1/2 tsp fennel seeds	• • • • •

Heat oil in pot on medium heat. Add garlic and onions and sauté for 3 minutes.

Add potatoes and sauté for 2 minutes. Stir in spinach, stock, saffron, thyme, fennel and lemon rind. Bring to boil, reduce heat and simmer for 15 to 20 minutes or until potatoes are soft. Season well with salt and pepper.

Combine sour cream with lemon juice and rind. Stir in parsley. Top each serving with 1 tbsp garnish.

SAFFRON

Saffron is the most expensive spice in the world. It comes from the stigmas of crocuses. Buy the yellow-red threads, which have more flavor than the powdered form and cannot be as easily adulterated. Saffron gives food a distinctive yellow color and an intense flavor.

ONION BISQUE WITH CHILI OIL

SERVES 6

This combination of sweet onions and hot spice makes a superb soup. As an alternative to the chili oil, you can simply grate Monterey Jack or Cheddar cheese on top and broil lightly. Chili oil can be purchased at Italian grocery stores, or you can make your own.

2 tbsp olive oil	1 tbsp balsamic vinegar
1 red onion, thinly sliced	½ tsp dried thyme
1 sweet onion, thinly sliced	5 cups chicken stock
2 leeks, trimmed and thinly sliced	¼ cup whipping cream
1 tsp chopped garlic	Salt and freshly ground pepper to taste
Pinch granulated sugar	3 tbsp ginger chili oil (page 6)

Heat oil in large pot on medium heat. Add onions, leeks, garlic and sugar. Sauté gently for 5 minutes or until onions are slightly softened.

Add vinegar and thyme and continue to cook, stirring occasionally, until onions are very soft but not colored, about 20 minutes.

Add stock and bring to boil. Reduce heat and simmer for 10 minutes.

Puree in food processor or with hand blender. Return to pot and add cream. Simmer for 5 minutes. Season well with salt and pepper.

Ladle soup into bowls and drizzle with chili oil.

CHILLED PEA SOUP WITH MINT

SERVES 4

Pea purees are all the rage; they are served both as soups and sauces. This bright green soup should be well pureed for the best taste and texture. Thawed frozen peas can also be used but will need only 5 minutes of cooking.

4 green onions, chopped

2 cups shelled green peas (about 1 lb in the pod)

20 mint leaves

3 cups chicken stock

1/4 cup whipping cream

Salt and freshly ground pepper to taste

1/4 cup chopped chives

. . . . .

Place green onions, peas, mint and stock in pot. Bring to boil, reduce heat and simmer for 10 minutes or until peas are tender.

Puree in food processor or with hand blender. Return to pot, add cream and simmer for 5 minutes. Season with salt and pepper and chill. Scatter with chives before serving.

RIBOLLITA

This robust bean and bread soup is a Tuscan specialty similar to minestrone. Serve it with a sprinkling of pepper and olive oil.

I prefer to serve ribollita as a soup poured over bread, but traditionally the bread and soup are layered in the pot and simmered for 20 minutes, or until the bread dissolves into the soup.

3 tbsp olive oil	2 28-oz (796 mL) cans diced tomatoes with juices
1 cup diced onions	2 cups vegetable stock or chicken stock
1 cup diced carrots	¼ tsp hot red pepper flakes
1 cup diced zucchini	Salt and freshly ground pepper to taste
2 tsp chopped garlic	8 slices stale Italian bread, toasted
2 cups diced unpeeled red potatoes	1 clove garlic, halved
8 cups sliced Swiss chard or kale	1 sweet onion, thinly sliced
1 tsp dried thyme	• • • • •
2 19-oz (540 mL) cans white kidney beans, rinsed and drained	

Heat oil in large pot on medium heat. Add onions, carrots, zucchini and garlic and sauté for 5 minutes or until softened.

Add potatoes, chard and thyme. Simmer for 5 minutes.

Puree one can of beans. Stir pureed beans, tomatoes and their juices into pot. Add stock and hot pepper flakes. Bring to boil, reduce heat and simmer, covered, for 40 minutes or until everything is soft.

Add remaining can of beans and cook for 10 minutes longer, uncovered. Season well with salt and pepper.

Rub bread with garlic clove and place in bottom of soup bowls. Pour hot soup over bread. Sprinkle with sliced onion.

CHILLED TOMATO SOUP WITH SPICES

SERVES 4 TO 6

This soup has the subtle flavors of lemon, lime and ginger and is incredibly refreshing. Make it in the summer with vine-ripened tomatoes at their juicy peak (use a little less honey if your tomatoes are very sweet).

1 tbsp olive oil	1/4 cup chopped fresh coriander
2 tsp chopped lemon grass	1/4 cup chopped fresh basil
2 tsp grated ginger	1/4 cup lime juice
2 tsp finely chopped garlic	1 tsp grated lime rind
2 cups chicken stock	Salt and freshly ground pepper to taste
1 tbsp honey	2 tbsp balsamic vinegar
3 lb tomatoes	1/2 cup sliced arugula
1/4 cup chopped fresh mint	4 yellow cherry tomatoes, quartered

Heat oil in small pot over medium-low heat. Add lemon grass and ginger, pressing slightly to release juices. Add garlic and sauté for about 2 minutes.

Add stock and honey and simmer for about 10 minutes. Remove from heat and strain liquid into large bowl. Discard solids. Let broth chill.

Chop tomatoes roughly and add to food processor. Add 3 tbsp each mint, coriander and basil, lime juice and rind and puree until smooth.

Strain tomato mixture into large bowl with broth, pressing on solids to release all the juice. Mix together and season with salt and pepper. Chill soup for at least 4 hours.

Stir in balsamic vinegar when ready to serve. Ladle soup into bowls and garnish with remaining fresh herbs, arugula and cherry tomatoes.

CHAPTER 3

Slow and Fast

Cooking is like love. It should be entered into with abandon or not at all.

– Harriet Van Horne

SLOW-COOKED SALMON

SERVES 4

This slow method of cooking salmon produces a fish that is very evenly cooked and moist throughout. Once the hot marinade has been poured over, bake the salmon immediately. Serve with Celery Root Mashed Potatoes (page 172) and green beans.

4 6-oz salmon fillets	½ cup sliced onions
Salt and freshly ground pepper to taste	½ tsp cracked peppercorns
1 cup white wine	2 tbsp olive oil
3 tbsp lemon juice	½ cup whipping cream
2 tbsp chopped fresh tarragon, dill or chervil,	2 tbsp finely chopped parsley
or 1 tsp dried	. . . . .

Preheat oven to 250 F.

Season salmon with salt and pepper and place in ovenproof baking dish.

Combine wine, lemon juice, tarragon, onions, peppercorns and olive oil in small pot. Bring to boil, reduce heat and simmer until reduced by half, about 3 to 5 minutes. Pour over salmon.

Bake salmon for 30 minutes, basting once, until fish is just cooked.

Place salmon on serving plate. Pour basting liquid into pot on high heat. Reduce until about ¼ cup remains.

Pour in cream, bring to boil and boil until thickened, about 3 to 4 minutes. Drizzle over salmon before serving. Garnish with parsley.

ROASTED SEA BASS WITH BRAISED LENTILS

SERVES 6 TO 8

You can also use frozen or canned lentils in this dish, but try to use the tiny, nutty-tasting French lentils de Puy, which have a lot of texture. If they are not available, use regular green lentils (red lentils will turn to mush). Serve with Saffron Aioli (page 94).

1 tbsp olive oil	TOPPING
1 onion, chopped	1/2 cup dried breadcrumbs
1/2 tsp chopped garlic	3 tbsp chopped fresh parsley
1 1/2 cups dried green lentils	1/2 tsp chopped garlic
1 bay leaf	2 tbsp olive oil
Pinch dried thyme	· · · · ·
Salt and freshly ground pepper to taste	GARNISH
1/2 cup chicken stock or water	2 tbsp chopped parsley
4 oz bacon, diced	· · · · ·
4 6-oz sea bass fillets	

Heat olive oil in pot on medium heat. Add onion and garlic and sauté for 3 minutes or until beginning to soften. Stir in lentils, bay leaf and thyme. Season with salt and pepper.

Add enough water to cover lentils by **1/2** inch. Bring to boil, reduce heat, cover and simmer until lentils are cooked, about 30 to 40 minutes. Drain off any water. Taste and adjust seasonings.

Preheat oven to 350 F.

Combine lentils with chicken stock in roasting pan. Sprinkle half the diced bacon over lentils. Top with sea bass fillets. Season with salt and pepper.

Combine breadcrumbs, parsley, garlic and olive oil for topping and spread over fish. Scatter over remaining bacon.

Bake for 25 to 30 minutes or until white juices begin to rise. Place sea bass on serving platter and spoon lentils on either side. Sprinkle with parsley.

SCOTTISH CHICKEN WITH LEEKS AND WHISKY

SERVES 4

This succulent chicken makes a fine main course for entertaining. It is a kind of Scottish coq au vin (use Port instead of Scotch for a Spanish version). Serve it with Cabbage with Sweet Onions and Balsamic (page 164) and mashed potatoes to soak up the sauce. Use a blended whisky rather than a single malt.

1 3-lb roasting chicken	¼ cup Scotch whisky
Salt and freshly ground pepper to taste	½ cup chicken stock
1 tbsp olive oil	½ cup whipping cream
2 tbsp butter	1 tsp grated lemon rind
3 leeks, trimmed and sliced	2 tbsp chopped fresh parsley

Preheat oven to 400 F.

Season chicken with salt and pepper.

Heat oil and butter in skillet on medium heat. Brown chicken, breast side down, for 3 minutes. Turn and brown remaining sides for about 3 minutes per side. Remove chicken and drain off all but 1 tbsp fat.

Add leeks to skillet and sauté for 3 minutes. Add Scotch and reduce by half to burn off alcohol. Add stock. Transfer leek mixture and chicken breast side up to an ovenproof baking dish.

Bake, covered, for 50 to 60 minutes, basting occasionally.

Remove chicken from baking dish and keep warm. Skim fat from sauce. Transfer sauce to pot, then add cream and lemon rind and bring to boil on high heat. Cook until slightly thickened, about 3 minutes. Season well with salt and pepper and stir in parsley.

Carve chicken and serve with sauce.

CLEANING LEEKS

To clean regular leeks, slice lengthwise down to but not through the root and rinse in warm water to dislodge any soil between the leaves. Trim off the roots and tough dark-green leaves.

PERFECT ROAST DUCK

SERVES 2 TO 4

Most people are afraid to cook duck because of its high fat content, but in fact duck has fewer calories than meat if you don't eat the skin. I like to slow-roast duck. The skin becomes so crisp that it crackles in your mouth, the meat is juicy and tender, and all the duck fat stays behind in the roasting pan, not under the skin. (And the fat does not splatter all over the oven!)

1 5-lb duck	1 tbsp balsamic vinegar
2 tbsp soy sauce	Salt and freshly ground pepper to taste

Preheat oven to 275 F.

Wash duck and pat dry. Prick skin all over with fork to help release fat. Place on rack in roasting pan.

Combine soy sauce and vinegar and brush over duck. Season with salt and pepper. Bake for 3 hours.

Increase temperature to 375 F and bake for 45 minutes or until juices run clear and skin is crisp. Place duck on carving board and let sit for 10 minutes before carving.

DUCK

There are many benefits to cooking your own duck. Duck fat makes the best fried potatoes ever. Duck skin, re-crisped in the oven, can be sprinkled over a salad. The carcass makes a strong broth, and leftover duck stir-fried with onions, carrots and ginger makes a juicy filling for a spring roll or iceberg lettuce wrap.

To carve a duck, cut it in quarters with kitchen shears. For a more elegant presentation, slice down between the thigh bone and the carcass and remove the leg and thigh in one piece. With the tip of a sharp knife, cut along the breast at the breast bone and scrape it off the bone, removing it along with the wing.

A large duck (more than 5 lbs) will serve four; a small duck will serve two.

BRAISED BEEF WITH ROOT VEGETABLES

SERVES 6

A hearty one-dish meal that can also be made with pork. This tastes even better the day after it is made. The marrow bone adds flavor to the broth. Scoop out the marrow at the end of the cooking time and stir it into the stew.

2 lb stewing beef	2 cups beef stock
Salt and freshly ground pepper to taste	1 marrow bone, optional
1 tsp dried thyme	4 cups peeled and diced rutabaga
3 tbsp vegetable oil or bacon fat	4 large red potatoes, cut in eighths
3 cups thinly sliced onions	8 cups thinly sliced green cabbage
2 cups chopped carrots	2 tbsp slivered fresh basil
½ cup red wine	· · · · ·

Preheat oven to 325 F.

Season beef with salt, pepper and thyme.

Heat 2 tbsp oil in skillet on high heat. Add beef a few pieces at a time and brown well on each side, about 1 minute per side. Reserve. Continue with remaining beef, adding oil if needed.

Reduce heat to medium and add remaining 1 tbsp oil. Add onions and sauté until slightly browned, about 3 minutes. Add carrots and sauté until coated with oil. Add wine, stock and marrow bone. Bring to boil, stirring.

Transfer meat and vegetable mixture to ovenproof baking dish. Cover and bake for 1 hour. Add rutabaga and potatoes. Cover and bake for 30 minutes. Sprinkle cabbage on top, cover again and bake for 20 to 30 minutes or until cabbage is crisp-tender, rutabaga is soft and meat is tender. If broth is thin, cook uncovered on stove to reduce slightly. Taste and adjust seasonings if necessary. Sprinkle with basil before serving.

FAMILY-STYLE SHORTRIBS

SERVES 6

These tasty, meaty shortribs are superb. It is easier to remove the fat if the dish is made a day ahead and cooled. Serve with a salad and mashed potatoes.

6 racks beef shortribs	1 tsp chopped garlic
1/4 cup all-purpose flour	1/2 cup red wine
1 tsp dried thyme	6 canned or fresh tomatoes, chopped
Salt and freshly ground pepper to taste	3 cups beef stock
2 tbsp vegetable oil	1 bay leaf
1 large onion, chopped	1/4 cup finely chopped parsley

Preheat oven to 325 F.

Trim fat from top of each shortrib. Combine flour, thyme, salt and pepper and coat short-ribs with seasoned flour.

Heat oil in large skillet on high heat. Brown ribs on all sides until dark brown, about 2 minutes per side. Place ribs in ovenproof baking dish.

Reduce heat to medium and add onion and garlic to skillet. Sauté until onion softens slightly, about 2 minutes. Pour in wine, bring to boil and reduce until 1 tbsp remains.

Add tomatoes, stock and bay leaf. Bring to boil. Pour liquid over ribs and bake, covered, for 1 1/2 hours or until meat is tender.

Remove meat from ovenproof baking dish and skim fat from gravy. Transfer gravy to pot. Bring gravy to boil and cook on stove on high heat until liquid has reduced by one-third. Season to taste. Cut shortribs into chunks before serving, if desired. Sprinkle with parsley.

ITALIAN BEEF STEW

SERVES 4 TO 6

A rich stew that should leave enough to provide a second meal as a beef ragu sauce. To turn it into ragu, dice the cooked meat and return to the sauce. Serve with penne or other short pasta.

1 oz dried mushrooms	1 tbsp chopped fresh thyme or 1 tsp dried
1 cup boiling water	1 bay leaf
2 tbsp olive oil or vegetable oil	1 cup red wine
2 lb stewing beef, cut in 2-inch cubes	1 cup beef stock
Salt and freshly ground pepper to taste	1 28-oz (796 mL) can tomatoes,
1 onion, chopped	drained and chopped
2 carrots, chopped	1 tsp hot red pepper flakes, or to taste
1 stalk celery, chopped	1 tbsp red wine vinegar
2 tsp chopped garlic	• • • • •

Soak mushrooms in boiling water for 20 minutes or until softened. Strain mushrooms, reserving liquid.

Preheat oven to 325 F.

Heat oil in skillet on high heat. When oil is very hot, add meat a few cubes at a time and brown well, about 1 minute per side. Remove to plate and season with salt and pepper. Continue until all meat is browned.

Reduce heat to medium and add onion, carrots and celery. Sauté for 2 minutes or until onions are slightly softened. Add garlic, thyme and bay leaf. Sauté for 1 minute.

Add wine and bring to boil. Stir in stock, reserved mushroom liquid, tomatoes and hot pepper flakes. Simmer for 10 minutes. Transfer to ovenproof baking dish along with meat.

Cover and bake for 1½ hours. Add mushrooms and vinegar. Cook covered for 30 minutes or until meat is tender.

ZESTY BEEF AND MUSHROOM PIE

SERVES 4

Meat pies are real comfort food. Make this one ahead and reheat when needed. The beef stew can also be served without the pastry topping.
The dried mushrooms will give this dish extra mushroom flavor, but they can be omitted.

½ oz dried mushrooms	1 tsp chopped garlic
1 cup boiling water	2 tsp chopped fresh rosemary or ½ tsp dried
1 tsp dried thyme	¼ cup all-purpose flour
1 tbsp paprika	½ cup red wine
Pinch cayenne	1½ cups beef stock
Salt and freshly ground pepper to taste	1 tbsp butter
1 lb stewing beef, cut in 1-inch pieces	8 oz fresh mushrooms, trimmed and cut in half if large
2 tbsp olive oil	1 package frozen puff pastry, defrosted
1 onion, chopped	1 egg, beaten with a pinch of salt

Cover dried mushrooms with boiling water. Soak for 20 minutes or until softened. Strain, reserving mushrooms and liquid separately.

Preheat oven to 325 F.

Combine thyme, paprika, cayenne, salt and pepper. Toss meat with half of mixture. Reserve remaining mixture.

Heat oil in skillet on high heat. Add meat in batches (do not crowd pan) and brown on all sides. Reserve and continue until all meat is browned, adding oil if needed.

Reduce heat to medium and add onion and garlic. Sauté until softened, about 2 minutes. Stir in reserved spice mixture, rosemary and flour. Cook, stirring, until flour is pale gold, 2 to 3 minutes.

Pour in wine and bring to boil, stirring. Add stock and reserved mushroom liquid. Bring to boil.

Transfer meat and sauce to ovenproof baking dish, cover and bake until meat is just tender, about 2 hours.

Heat butter in skillet on medium-high heat. Add fresh and dried mushrooms and sauté for 3 minutes or until softened. Season well with salt and pepper. Combine with meat. Cool.

Place mixture in deep-dish pie plate or ovenproof baking dish. Roll out half of pastry until 1½ inches larger than dish (reserve remaining pastry for another use). Cut 1-inch strip from edges of pastry.

Brush edge of dish with water and lay strips of pastry on edges. Brush with beaten egg. Lay pastry on top, sealing edges. Cut steam hole and brush top with egg.

Bake for 30 minutes or until pastry is golden and filling is hot.

SLOW-COOKED BRISKET

SERVES 10

This beef brisket is the most succulent one I make. The secret is cooking the brisket slowly with a ton of onions and no liquid for the first hour.

I prefer to use double briskets; they have more fat, which can be easily removed when the brisket is chilled.

If you wish, you can add carrots and potatoes for the last 1½ hours of cooking.

5 lb beef brisket	10 cups chopped onions
¼ cup Dijon mustard	12 cloves garlic, peeled
1 tbsp cracked pepper	2 cups beef stock or chicken stock
Kosher salt to taste	3 tbsp tomato paste
1 tbsp paprika	2 tbsp chopped parsley
¼ cup olive oil	• • • • •

Preheat oven to 325 F.

Brush brisket with mustard. Sprinkle with pepper, salt and paprika.

Place 3 tbsp oil in large roasting pan on medium-high heat. Add brisket and sear on each side for about 2 minutes per side. Remove meat to baking sheet. Reduce heat to medium and stir in remaining 1 tbsp oil and onions.

Cook onions until pale-gold and tender, about 10 minutes. Stir in garlic. Place brisket on top of onions. Cover tightly and bake for 1 hour.

Stir in stock and tomato paste. Cover and cook for 1½ to 2 hours or until meat is very tender. Remove from oven and cool.

Discard fat that forms on top of gravy. Slice brisket against grain. Return brisket slices to gravy and reheat in liquid on top of stove or in a 325 F oven for 30 minutes. Taste and adjust seasonings and sprinkle with parsley before serving.

ROAST LAMB FROM UMBRIA

SERVES 6

This fragrant dish is adapted from a traditional Umbrian recipe. Use lots of fresh herbs, but don't chop them.

1 3-lb boneless leg of lamb, butterflied	1/4 cup loosely packed fresh mint leaves
2 cups beef stock or chicken stock	1/4 cup fresh rosemary leaves
1 head garlic, separated in cloves	2 tbsp fresh thyme leaves
1/4 cup loosely packed fresh sage leaves	Salt and freshly ground pepper to taste

Preheat oven to 450 F.

Trim lamb of any fat and season with salt and pepper. If meat is very uneven, place between two sheets of waxed paper and pound to even thickness.

Remove root end from garlic cloves. Place stock and garlic cloves in small pot. Bring to simmer and cook for 10 minutes or until garlic is soft. Strain stock and reserve. Peel garlic cloves.

Lay lamb flat with long side toward you. Strew with all herbs and season with salt and pepper. Lay garlic cloves down middle of lamb, parallel to long side. Roll up lamb lengthwise. Skewer together or sew together with trussing needle and string. Tie in a few places. Season well with salt and pepper.

Place lamb seam side down in roasting pan. Roast for 10 minutes. Reduce heat to 300 F. Pour reserved stock around lamb and cook for 1 hour and 15 minutes or until juices are just pink. Add more stock if needed.

Remove roast from oven and let sit for 10 minutes. Carve into thin slices and serve with pan juices.

CHARLEVOIX LAMB LEG

SERVES 6 TO 8

Superb slow-cooked lamb for the oven or barbecue. If you want to grill it, grill by the indirect method, with one burner left on and the lamb sitting on the turned-off side. Serve with mint jelly. If you wish, you can add chunks of unpeeled Yukon Gold potatoes and let them cook with the lamb in the oven.

1 tsp chopped garlic	1 tbsp chopped fresh marjoram or 1 tsp dried
2 tbsp Dijon mustard	1 tbsp chopped fresh lemon thyme or 1 tsp dried
2 tbsp chopped pickled ginger	2 tbsp olive oil
1 tbsp Indian curry powder	Salt to taste
2 tbsp chopped fresh rosemary or 2 tsp dried	1 4- to 5-lb leg of lamb, bone-in

Combine garlic, mustard, ginger, curry powder, rosemary, marjoram, thyme, oil and salt. Spread over lamb and marinate for 1 hour at room temperature or refrigerate overnight.

Preheat oven to 450 F.

Place lamb on rack in roasting pan. Bake for 15 minutes. Reduce heat to 300 F and bake for 2 hours for medium-rare.

Place lamb on carving board. Starting at thick end, slice at 45-degree angle to bone. Turn lamb over and slice other side.

MINT JELLY

Coarsely chop 2 cups tightly packed mint leaves in food processor or by hand. Combine with 2 cups water in pot. Bring to boil, stirring occasionally. Reduce heat and simmer for 5 minutes. Remove from heat and let stand for 2 hours or until cool. Strain mixture through fine sieve or cheesecloth, pressing down on mint.

Measure 1 3/4 cups mint liquid into pot. Add 1/4 cup lime juice and 3 1/2 cups granulated sugar. Bring to boil, stirring occasionally. Add 1/2 cup liquid pectin. Return to boil, boil for 1 minute and remove from heat.

Skim foam from jelly. Place in sterilized jars and cap with sterilized lids. For more immediate use, place in clean jars and refrigerate for up to 1 month.

Makes about 3 cups.

NEW IRISH STEW

SERVES 6 TO 8

Here is a contemporary version of Irish stew made with ground lamb instead of mutton chops.

1 tbsp vegetable oil	1 tbsp Dijon mustard
1 large onion, thinly sliced	Salt and freshly ground pepper to taste
2 lb ground lamb	3 lb red potatoes, thinly sliced
1 tbsp chopped fresh rosemary or 1 tsp dried	4 cloves garlic, thinly sliced
½ cup red wine	2 tbsp butter
2 cups chopped canned tomatoes	1 cup grated Cheddar cheese
1 tbsp Worcestershire sauce	• • • • •

Heat oil in large skillet on medium heat. Add onion and sauté for 5 minutes. Remove and reserve.

Add lamb to skillet and sauté until lamb loses its pinkness, about 5 minutes. Add rosemary, wine, tomatoes, Worcestershire and mustard. Bring to boil. Reduce heat and simmer for 10 minutes, or until sauce reduces and thickens slightly. Season with salt and pepper.

Preheat oven to 375 F.

Toss potato slices with salt and pepper.

Layer one-third of potatoes, half the garlic, half the onions and half the lamb in buttered baking dish. Top with one-third more potatoes and remaining garlic, onions and lamb. Finish with remaining potatoes. Dot with butter.

Bake, covered, for 30 minutes. Uncover, sprinkle with cheese and bake for 30 minutes longer or until potatoes are tender.

BRAISED LAMB SHANKS WITH MIDDLE EASTERN SPICES

SERVES 6

Lamb shanks are very trendy because they are full of flavor and are meltingly tender when they have been cooked slowly. The sauce for this dish is rich, thick and spicy. Stir in the Vegetable Garnish or serve separately.

2 tsp ground cumin	1 onion, coarsely chopped
2 tsp dried ground ginger	1/2 cup coarsely chopped carrots
2 tsp dried ground coriander	1/2 cup coarsely chopped celery
2 tsp paprika	1 cup pureed canned tomatoes
1/2 tsp cinnamon	2 cups beef stock
1/2 tsp cayenne	1 tsp dried thyme
6 lamb shanks	1 bay leaf
3 tbsp olive oil	4 cups Vegetable Garnish
Salt and freshly ground pepper to taste	• • • • •

Preheat oven to 300 F. Combine cumin, ginger, coriander, paprika, cinnamon and cayenne. Toss lamb shanks with 2 tsp spice mixture, reserving remaining spice mixture.

Heat 2 tbsp oil in skillet on medium-high heat. Brown lamb shanks in batches on all sides, about 2 minutes per side. Reserve lamb and season with salt and pepper. Wipe out skillet.

Add remaining 1 tbsp oil to skillet on medium heat. Add onion, carrots and celery. Sauté until onion is slightly browned, about 5 minutes. Add remaining spice mixture and sauté for 30 seconds. Add tomatoes, stock, thyme and bay leaf and bring to boil. Transfer meat and sauce to ovenproof baking dish.

Bake, covered, for 2 hours or until meat is tender and nearly falling off bone. Remove meat. Skim fat, then remove vegetables with slotted spoon. Discard bay leaf.

Puree vegetables in food processor or with hand blender. Stir back into baking dish and simmer until sauce reduces and lightly coats a spoon, about 10 minutes. Return lamb to pot and add Vegetable Garnish. Simmer for 15 minutes.

VEGETABLE GARNISH

This garnish can be served with lamb or chicken.

Heat 2 tbsp olive oil in skillet on medium-high heat. Add 3 cups diced zucchini and 1/2 cup each chopped red and yellow pepper. Sauté until vegetables are crisp-tender, about 5 to 8 minutes. Stir in 1/2 cup raisins. Season with salt and freshly ground pepper to taste.

Makes about 4 cups.

CRUSTY RICE AND LAMB TAGINE

SERVES 4 TO 6

This textured, magnificent one-dish meal has a crisp layer of rice topping fragrant lamb and a soft, steamy rice layer on the bottom. The seasonings are Iranian. The dish can be made ahead of time and reheated efore unmolding. You can alter the filling by using ground beef or chicken instead of lamb.

2 cups basmati rice	1 tsp cinnamon
2 1/2 cups cold water	1/4 tsp cayenne or to taste
Salt and freshly ground pepper to taste	3 cups sliced spinach
1/4 cup chopped fresh coriander	2 tbsp chopped fresh mint
1 tbsp olive oil	1/2 cup chopped dried apricots
2 cups chopped onions	1/2 cup pine nuts
1 1/2 lb ground lamb	1 tbsp lemon juice
1 tbsp chopped garlic	3 tbsp butter
2 tsp paprika	• • • • •

Wash rice in cool running water. Place rice in pot with cold water and bring to boil. Reduce heat, cover and simmer for 15 to 20 minutes or until rice is tender. Season with salt and pepper and stir in coriander.

Heat oil in 10-inch non-stick skillet on medium heat. Add onions and sauté until softened, about 3 minutes. Add lamb, garlic, paprika, cinnamon and cayenne. Sauté for 5 minutes or until lamb is cooked. Season with salt and pepper.

Add spinach to skillet and stir-fry until spinach wilts, about 1 to 2 minutes. Stir in mint, apricots, pine nuts and lemon juice. Cook for 1 minute and reserve. Wipe out skillet.

Melt butter in same skillet. Remove from heat and add half the rice, spreading it evenly over bottom and up sides of skillet. Top with all of lamb mixture. Finish with remaining rice, sealing in lamb mixture. Make hole down through center of mixture with a wooden spoon.

Cover skillet. Place on very low heat and cook for 35 minutes. Loosen sides of rice. Set bottom of skillet in cold water for 2 minutes to help loosen crust. Uncover, place a serving plate on top of rice and unmold mixture onto plate, crusty side up.

HONEY GARLIC SPARERIBS

SERVES 4

Honey garlic spareribs were a staple of our Chinese take-out dinners when I was growing up, so this is a re-creation of what is a comfort food for my family. Back ribs are meatier than side ones and a better choice for this dish. Serve with garlic scapes if available.

3 lb back spareribs	2 tbsp chopped garlic
Salt and freshly ground pepper to taste	1 tbsp grated ginger
1/4 cup honey	2 tbsp brown sugar
1/4 cup rice wine or white wine	3 tbsp hoisin sauce
2 tbsp soy sauce	1 tsp Asian chili sauce
1/4 cup rice wine vinegar	1/2 cup chicken stock or water

Trim spareribs and cut into racks of three ribs each. Place in roasting pan and season with salt and pepper.

Combine honey, rice wine, soy sauce, vinegar, garlic, ginger, sugar, hoisin and chili sauce and pour over ribs. Marinate for 1 hour at room temperature or refrigerate for up to 8 hours, turning occasionally.

Preheat oven to 375 F.

Stir stock into marinade and bake ribs uncovered for 1 hour or until tender, turning every 20 minutes and brushing with marinade. If marinade becomes too dry, add more stock or water; if it is too thin, reduce on stove over medium-high heat (the sauce should be thick but pourable).

Place ribs on platter. Pour sauce over ribs.

BRAISED PORK WITH BALSAMIC VINEGAR

SERVES 6 TO 8

Braised on top of the stove in the Italian manner, this pork is juicy and flavorful with a dark, slightly tart sauce.

I use the leaner end of the pork loin in this recipe. Serve with roasted red potatoes and rapini.

1 3-lb pork loin roast	1 onion, sliced
1 clove garlic, cut in half	2 tsp dried rosemary
Salt and freshly ground pepper to taste	1/4 cup red wine
2 tbsp olive oil	1/4 cup balsamic vinegar
1 tbsp butter	1 1/2 cups chicken stock

Rub pork with cut side of garlic and then chop garlic. Season pork with salt and pepper.

Heat oil and butter in pot on medium heat (pot should be large enough to hold roast). Add roast and brown slowly on all sides, about 5 minutes per side. Remove from pot.

Add onion, rosemary and chopped garlic to pot and sauté for 2 minutes. Add wine and bring to boil, scraping up any bits on bottom of pot.

Return roast to pot, reduce heat and simmer for 10 minutes to allow some evaporation of liquid. Cover.

Combine vinegar and stock in bowl. Turn roast and baste with 1/4 cup vinegar mixture every 15 minutes. Keep the roast moist but not wet. Cook for 1 1/4 to 1 1/2 hours or until pork is tender and juices are clear.

Remove pork and keep warm. If pan juices are watery, boil down until strongly flavored, adding any remaining vinegar and stock mixture. Slice pork and serve with sauce.

SCOTTISH MEATLOAF

SERVES 4 TO 6

This is a traditional Scottish recipe. Using oats instead of breadcrumbs results in a super-moist meatloaf. This dish needs lots of seasoning, so cook a small portion before shaping the loaf to taste for seasoning.

1/2 cup quick-cooking oats	1/2 tsp dried marjoram
3 tbsp milk or water	1 egg, beaten
3/4 lb ground veal	Salt and freshly ground pepper to taste
3/4 lb ground beef	1 tbsp ketchup
1/2 cup grated carrots	1 tbsp HP sauce
1 cup finely chopped onions	Dash hot red pepper sauce or to taste
1 tsp dried thyme	• • • • •

Preheat oven to 350 F.

Combine oats, milk, veal, beef, carrots, onions, thyme, marjoram and egg in bowl. Season with salt and pepper. Spoon into oiled baking dish and form into rectangular meat-loaf shape about 2 inches high. (This allows for more even cooking.)

Bake for 30 minutes.

Combine ketchup, HP sauce and hot pepper sauce. Make three slits in top of meatloaf. Brush all sides with sauce, making sure some gets into slits.

Bake for 20 to 30 minutes or until juices run clear. Let sit for 5 minutes to allow juices to retract before slicing.

OSSO BUCO

SERVES 4

For a smoother, thicker texture, you can puree the sauce in a food processor, then pour it back over the shanks. Add a few drops of hot pepper sauce, if desired.

4 veal shanks, 1¹/₂ inches thick	2 cups chicken stock or veal stock
Salt and freshly ground pepper to taste	1 bay leaf
2 tbsp olive oil	2 stalks parsley
1 cup chopped onions	• • • • •
1 cup chopped carrots	GREMOLATA
¹/₂ cup chopped celery	1 tsp finely chopped garlic
1 tsp chopped garlic	¹/₄ cup finely chopped parsley
1 cup white wine	1 tsp grated lemon rind
1¹/₂ cups chopped canned tomatoes	¹/₂ tsp finely chopped fresh rosemary or pinch dried

Preheat oven to 325 F. Season shanks with salt and pepper.

Heat oil in skillet on high heat. Add shanks and brown well on each side, about 2 minutes per side. Remove from skillet.

Reduce heat to medium. Add onions, carrots, celery and garlic and sauté until softened, about 2 minutes.

Pour in wine and bring to boil, scraping up any bits on bottom of skillet. Stir in tomatoes, stock, bay leaf and parsley stalks and bring to boil. Place shanks in overproof baking dish in single layer. Pour over liquid (liquid should come three-quarters of way up shanks). Add more stock if needed.

Bake, covered, for 1¹/₂ to 2 hours or until shanks are fork-tender.

Combine garlic, parsley, lemon rind and rosemary for gremolata.

Remove shanks from liquid with slotted spoon and reserve. Remove bay leaf and parsley stalks. If sauce is too thin, bring to boil on stove on high heat and reduce until slightly thickened. Pour sauce over shanks and sprinkle with gremolata.

UMBRIAN RAGU

SERVES 2; SERVES 4 WITH PASTA

I could not understand why the market seller threw in a carrot and stalk of celery when we bought some tomatoes in the Umbrian market we visited — until I saw Umbrian ragu being made. Serve as a stew with bread or as a sauce with pasta, sprinkled with grated pecorino or Parmesan cheese.

¼ cup olive oil	1 tsp chopped fresh rosemary
2 cups chopped onions	or ¼ tsp dried
2 cups chopped canned or fresh tomatoes	1 tsp chopped fresh sage or ¼ tsp dried
1 large carrot, cut in quarters	1 tbsp chopped Italian parsley
1 stalk celery, cut in half	½ cup red wine
2 tsp chopped garlic	1 cup beef stock
8 oz ground veal or pork	Salt and freshly ground pepper to taste

Heat 2 tbsp oil in pot on medium heat. Add 1 cup chopped onions, reserving remainder. Sauté for 3 minutes or until softened. Stir in tomatoes and cook for 10 to 12 minutes or until thickened.

Heat remaining 2 tbsp olive oil in another large pot on medium heat. Add remaining onions, carrot, celery and garlic. Sauté for 3 minutes.

Stir in veal. Cook for 5 minutes or until veal loses its pinkness. Stir in rosemary, sage and parsley. Stir in wine and bring to boil.

Add tomato mixture and stock and return to boil.

Reduce heat, cover and cook for 1 hour or until sauce thickens. Season well with salt and pepper. Remove celery and carrot and discard.

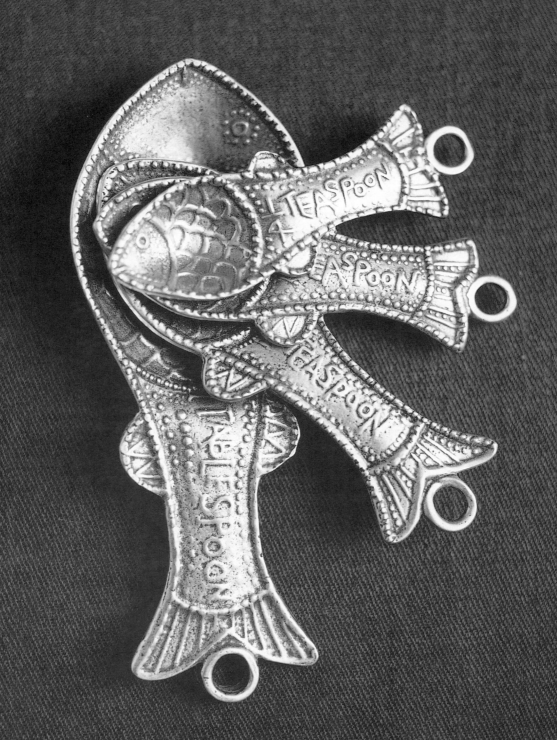

CHAPTER 4

Fish and Seafood

First food, then morality.
– Bertolt Brecht

COD IN SPICY SAUCE

SERVES 4

This is a great dish for entertaining because it looks and tastes sensational. Cod stands up to the rich and spicy Eastern Mediterranean sauce, but you could also use monkfish or grouper if desired. Serve with couscous.

3 tbsp olive oil	1 tbsp paprika
1 cup chopped onions	1/2 tsp cayenne
1/2 cup chopped fennel	Salt and freshly ground pepper to taste
1/2 cup chopped carrots	Pinch saffron threads, crushed
1 tbsp chopped garlic	1 tbsp chopped parsley
1 tbsp tomato paste	1 bay leaf
3 cups fish stock or chicken stock	1 1/2 lb cod fillets, cut in 2-inch squares
1 tsp ground cumin	1 lemon, quartered
1 tsp harissa (page 6) or Asian chili sauce	. . . . .

Heat oil in large skillet on high heat. Add onions, fennel and carrots and sauté for 2 minutes or until softened. Add garlic and sauté for 1 minute.

Combine tomato paste with 1/2 cup stock and add to skillet along with cumin, harissa, paprika, cayenne, salt and pepper. Bring to boil. Add remaining stock and cook over high heat for 8 to 10 minutes or until slightly thickened.

Add saffron, parsley and bay leaf. Reduce heat to medium-low and simmer for 10 minutes or until flavors are intense. Taste and adjust seasonings if necessary.

Add cod, cover and cook until cod releases its juices, about 5 to 8 minutes. Serve garnished with lemon wedges.

PAPRIKA

Paprika is a deep red, earthy spice made from peppers grown mainly in Hungary, Spain and the U.S. Its flavor ranges from mild and sweet to nearly as hot as cayenne. Hungarian paprika is the most common, and it is fairly bland. Spanish paprika is made from a slightly hotter pepper and can be quite smoky in flavor. If your paprika is not hot enough, add a pinch of cayenne.

ROASTED COD AND SHRIMP PROVENÇAL STYLE

SERVES 4

This is a sensational dish for a dinner party when you don't want to spend time in the kitchen. Serve it with roasted potatoes and Curried Green Beans (page 168). If you can't find herbes de Provence, you can make your own (page 5), or just use thyme, summer savory or fennel seeds.

2 tbsp grainy Dijon mustard	12 shrimp, shelled
2 tsp dried herbes de Provence	1½ cups seeded and diced fresh tomatoes
1 tsp chopped garlic	Salt and freshly ground pepper to taste
3 tbsp olive oil	¼ cup whipping cream
4 6-oz cod fillets	• • • • •

Combine mustard, 1 tsp herbes de Provence, garlic and 2 tbsp olive oil. Brush mixture on fish and shrimp. Marinate at room temperature for 30 minutes.

Preheat oven to 450 F.

Cover bottom of ovenproof baking dish with remaining 1 tbsp oil and place fish in center of dish. Scatter tomatoes and remaining 1 tsp herbes de Provence around fish. Season everything with salt and pepper.

Bake for 5 minutes. Add shrimp and bake for 5 to 8 minutes longer or until fish juices begin to rise. Remove shrimp and fish and keep warm.

Pour juices and tomatoes into small pot. Add cream. Bring to boil and boil for 2 minutes until slightly thickened. If you prefer a smooth sauce, whisk with a hand blender.

Serve cod and shrimp with sauce.

QUICK FISH IN THE FRENCH MANNER

SERVES 4

This is a very quick one-dish meal. Serve with a tomato and basil salad. Black cod, or sable fish, is a tasty, firm-fleshed fish that seems to have replaced sea bass on restaurant menus. Do not precook the spinach (baby spinach will cook in the moisture from the potatoes and the fish).

2 cups peeled and thinly sliced Yukon Gold potatoes	3 cups baby spinach
2 sprigs fresh thyme or 1/2 tsp dried	2 tbsp olive oil
4 cloves garlic, peeled	1 tbsp butter
1 cup water	1/4 cup grated Parmesan cheese
1 cup milk	1/4 cup pesto
Salt and freshly ground pepper to taste	4 6-oz black cod or grouper fillets

Preheat oven to 450 F.

Place potatoes, thyme and garlic in pot with water and milk to cover (add more water if necessary). Bring to boil, reduce heat, cover and simmer for 10 minutes or until potatoes are tender. Season with salt and pepper.

Drain potatoes and garlic, reserving 1/2 cup liquid, and spread half of potatoes in buttered baking dish. Top with spinach, sprinkle with 1 tbsp oil and top with remaining potatoes. Dot with butter, pour over reserved liquid, and sprinkle with Parmesan.

Combine remaining 1 tbsp oil with pesto and spread over fish. Place fish on top of potatoes.

Bake for 12 to 15 minutes or until white juices begin to appear. Serve fish on bed of potatoes and spinach.

PESTO

In food processor, combine 2 cloves garlic, 2 cups fresh basil leaves (packed), 2 tbsp pine nuts and 1/2 cup olive oil. Process until smooth. Season with salt and freshly ground pepper to taste. (Pesto can be frozen at this point.)

Before using, stir in 1/4 cup grated Parmesan cheese and 2 tbsp additional olive oil.

Makes about 1 1/2 cups.

GROUPER WITH CUBAN FLAVORINGS

SERVES 4

Serve this with rice, an avocado tomato salad and mojo — a spicy, orange-flavored hot sauce that can be bought at South American grocery stores. If you cannot find any, make your own or use a favorite hot sauce.

1 tsp grated lime rind	1/4 tsp hot red pepper flakes
2 tbsp lime juice	Salt to taste
1 tsp finely chopped garlic	2 tbsp olive oil
2 tbsp chopped fresh coriander	4 6-oz grouper fillets
2 tbsp chopped fresh basil	. . . . .

Combine lime rind, lime juice, garlic, coriander, basil, hot pepper flakes, salt and oil.

Place grouper in baking dish in single layer and coat with marinade. Marinate at room temperature for 30 minutes.

Preheat oven to 400 F.

Bake grouper for 15 to 20 minutes or until white juices begin to appear.

MOJO SAUCE

Combine 2 tbsp chopped parsley, 2 tbsp chopped fresh coriander, 2 tbsp finely chopped garlic, 1/4 cup fresh lime juice, 1/4 cup fresh orange juice and 1 tsp hot red pepper sauce. Add 1/2 cup very hot olive oil. Cool.

Makes about 1 1/4 cups.

HALIBUT WITH ANCHOVY GARLIC SAUCE

SERVES 4

Serve this with linguine or angelhair noodles and a green salad.

¼ cup olive oil

4 6-oz halibut fillets

Salt and freshly ground pepper to taste

6 cloves garlic, thinly sliced

8 anchovies, chopped

1 tsp hot red pepper flakes

¼ cup chopped parsley

2 cups seeded and diced plum tomatoes

Sprigs of chervil or parsley

· · · · ·

Heat 2 tbsp oil in skillet on high heat. Season halibut with salt and pepper. Sear fillets for 1 to 2 minutes per side or until golden. Turn fish, reduce heat to medium-low, cover pan and cook for 5 to 6 minutes or until fish is firm to the touch and white juices begin to appear.

Add remaining 2 tbsp oil to another skillet on medium-low heat. Add garlic, anchovies, hot pepper flakes and parsley. Simmer gently for 4 minutes or until garlic is pale gold and anchovies melt into sauce.

Add tomatoes and cook for 2 minutes. Season with salt and pepper.

Pour sauce over fish and garnish with chervil.

SAUTÉED HALIBUT WITH CONFIT SPICES

SERVES 4

Sautéing fish provides maximum flavor with a minimum of fuss. Here halibut is sautéed with the traditional French spicing usually used in confit of duck. Serve with Potato Pancakes (page 171) or Mushroom Risotto (page 145).

1 shallot, chopped	SALAD
2 tsp kosher salt	1 tbsp red wine vinegar
1 tbsp cracked peppercorns	1/4 tsp Dijon mustard
1 tsp dried thyme	3 tbsp olive oil
1 tsp finely chopped garlic	Salt and freshly ground pepper to taste
2 bay leaves, crumbled	1 bunch arugula
2 tbsp olive oil	• • • • •
4 6-oz halibut fillets	

Combine shallot, kosher salt, cracked peppercorns, thyme, garlic, bay leaves and 1 tbsp oil. Spread over fish and marinate at room temperature for 30 minutes.

Whisk together vinegar, mustard and 3 tbsp olive oil for salad. Season with salt and pepper. Toss dressing with arugula. Place on 4 individual plates.

Heat remaining 1 tbsp olive oil in skillet on medium heat. Add fish skin side down. Cook for 2 minutes. Cover, reduce heat to medium-low and cook for 5 to 6 minutes longer or until fish is firm to the touch and white juices begin to rise. Serve fish on bed of arugula.

MONKFISH CASSOULET

SERVES 4

Cassoulet is a rich dish of beans, pork and duck that simmers for hours. This extraordinary version uses monkfish, canned beans and pancetta. Monkfish should be cleaned and cut into medallions for this unusual dish that includes canned beans and cassoulet seasonings (using duck fat instead of olive oil will make it even better).

3 tbsp olive oil or duck fat	Salt and freshly ground pepper to taste
4 slices pancetta or bacon, chopped	· · · · ·
½ cup chopped shallots	TOPPING
1 tbsp chopped garlic	½ cup dry breadcrumbs
1 19-oz (540 mL) can Romano beans, rinsed and drained	2 tbsp chopped parsley
	1 tsp chopped garlic
1 cup chopped canned tomatoes, with juice	3 tbsp olive oil or duck fat
2 tbsp chopped parsley	· · · · ·
4 monkfish medallions, about 4 oz each, cut in half	

Preheat oven to 350 F.

Heat 1 tbsp oil in skillet on medium heat. Add pancetta, shallots and garlic and sauté for 3 minutes or until garlic is soft. Add beans and cook for 2 minutes. Add tomatoes and parsley and cook for 10 minutes.

Transfer beans to baking dish. Wipe out skillet.

Heat remaining 2 tbsp olive oil in skillet on medium-high heat. Season medallions with salt and pepper and cook for 1 minute per side. Place fish on top of beans.

Combine breadcrumbs, parsley, garlic and 3 tbsp olive oil for topping. Sprinkle topping over fish.

Bake for 20 to 25 minutes or until medallions are cooked and juices are white.

SIMPLY SALMON

SERVES 6

This is an easy salmon dish that can feed a crowd. For a larger group you can use a fillet as large as four pounds, but the timing will not change, as fish cooks by thickness, not weight (cook for 10 minutes per inch). One large piece looks spectacular on a buffet. Serve with Arugula Hollandaise.

2 tbsp olive oil

1 2-lb salmon fillet, skin removed

2 tbsp lemon juice

2 tbsp chopped fresh herbs (e.g., dill, tarragon, mint, thyme) or 2 tsp dried

Salt and freshly ground pepper to taste

Preheat oven to 450 F.

Place sheet of foil (large enough to enclose salmon) on baking sheet. Brush with a little oil. Place fish on top and brush with remaining oil. Sprinkle with lemon juice, herbs, salt and pepper. Fold up sides of foil to completely enclose fish.

Roast fish for 12 to 20 minutes, depending on thickness.

Remove fish from foil and slide onto serving platter along with any juice. Cut into serving pieces.

ARUGULA HOLLANDAISE

This is a quick, no-fail Hollandaise sauce. It can be made ahead and kept warm in a Thermos.

Place 1/2 cup butter in pot on medium heat and bring to boil. Meanwhile, combine 2 egg yolks, 2 cups arugula and 1/4 cup whipping cream in food processor. Pour bubbling butter slowly through feed tube while machine runs. Sauce will thicken. Turn off machine, stir in lemon juice, salt and freshly ground pepper to taste.

ROASTED SPICY SALMON WITH MANGO CORIANDER RELISH

SERVES 4

A zesty dish with an Indian flair. The marinade can also be used with chicken or lamb. Serve this with rice and Spinach and Rapini Sag (page 175). The relish can be made a day ahead. The salmon can be grilled or baked.

2 tsp chopped garlic	MANGO CORIANDER RELISH
1 tbsp grated ginger	1 large mango, peeled and diced
1 tbsp lemon juice	3 green onions, finely chopped
1 tbsp garam masala (page 5) or curry paste	1 tbsp grated ginger
2 tbsp vegetable oil	1 tsp finely chopped jalapeño pepper
1/4 cup yogurt	2 tbsp lime juice
4 6-oz salmon fillets	2 tbsp chopped fresh mint
Salt to taste	Salt to taste

Combine garlic, ginger, lemon juice, garam masala, oil, yogurt and salt. Place salmon in oiled baking dish and brush with marinade. Marinate at room temperature for 1 hour.

Combine mango, green onions, ginger, jalapeño, lime juice and mint for relish. Season with salt. Refrigerate until needed.

Preheat oven to 450 F.

Bake salmon for 10 to 12 minutes or until white juices just begin to appear.

Serve salmon with relish on the side.

SALMON WELLINGTON

SERVES 4

An update of the old favorite Beef Wellington, this memorable main course can be prepared a day ahead and refrigerated, but bring to room temperature before baking. Serve with sautéed peppers and sugarsnap peas.

8 chard leaves	SAUCE
2 tsp paprika	¼ cup chopped parsley
2 tsp ground cumin	¼ cup chopped fresh coriander
1 tsp dried ground ginger	½ tsp chopped garlic
Pinch cayenne	3 tbsp lemon juice
Salt to taste	¼ cup olive oil
4 6-oz salmon fillets, skin removed	Pinch cayenne
4 sheets phyllo pastry	Salt to taste
¼ cup butter, melted	• • • • •

Preheat oven to 400 F.

Bring pot of water to boil and immerse chard leaves. Boil for 1 minute and then drain. Refresh with cold water and drain again.

Combine paprika, cumin, ginger, cayenne and salt. Sprinkle over salmon. Dry chard with a paper towel and wrap each fillet in chard leaves.

Lay 1 sheet of phyllo on counter. Brush with butter. Lay one salmon fillet on top third of phyllo. Roll phyllo over salmon, fold in ends of phyllo envelope fashion, brush phyllo again and continue to roll. Place on oiled baking sheet and prepare remaining phyllo rolls. Brush tops of rolls with remaining melted butter.

Bake for 15 to 20 minutes or until phyllo is golden.

Make sauce while phyllo is baking. In food processor or blender combine parsley, coriander, garlic, lemon juice, olive oil and cayenne. Season with salt. Serve a spoonful of sauce beside each phyllo roll.

SWEET AND SOUR SALMON

Try serving this light and fresh pickled salmon with Cucumber Onion Salad (page 155) as a first course. It will keep in the refrigerator in the pickling liquid for at least one week.

2 cups white vinegar	2 tbsp mixed pickling spices
1 1/2 cups water	2 tbsp thinly sliced ginger
1/3 cup granulated sugar	6 bay leaves
2 tbsp kosher salt	2 onions, sliced 1/4 inch thick
2 lb salmon fillet, skin removed	• • • • •

Bring vinegar, water, sugar and salt to boil in pot. Let mixture cool completely.

Cut salmon into pieces approximately 1 x 2 inches. Place layer of salmon in glass bowl or plastic container. Sprinkle with pickling spices, ginger and bay leaves, a layer of onions, then another layer of salmon, spices and onions, continuing until you have used everything up.

Pour cooled marinade over fish to completely cover. Cover and refrigerate for 2 to 3 days before using.

VINE-WRAPPED GRILLED SALMON WITH VERJUS

SERVES 4

In this recipe the vine leaves seal in moisture and make it easier to turn the fish on the grill; they also provide a wonderful presentation. Use jarred vine leaves packed in brine, but rinse them before blanching.

Verjus, the juice of grapes, was used in cooking centuries before wine. Chefs like using it because it does not conflict with the taste of wine you are serving with the meal.

3 tbsp grainy Dijon mustard
3 tbsp soy sauce
2 tbsp olive oil
Freshly ground pepper to taste
1 2-lb salmon fillet, skin removed
Vine leaves

VERJUS BUTTER
8 oz seedless red grapes
¼ cup butter
Salt and freshly ground pepper to taste

· · · · ·

Combine mustard, soy sauce, oil and pepper. Spread over salmon.

Blanch vine leaves in boiling water for 2 minutes. Drain.

Lay overlapping vine leaves on baking sheet until you have enough to wrap salmon. Place salmon on leaves and fold leaves over fish. Lay more leaves on top if necessary to completely encase salmon. Wind string around to secure package.

Puree grapes in food processor or blender. Press pulp through sieve. You should have about ½ cup juice.

Bring juice to boil in small pot and reduce until about ⅓ cup remains and juice starts to thicken. Whisk in butter, letting sauce boil (it will thicken). Season with salt and pepper.

Place salmon on grill on high heat and cook, covered, for 7 minutes per side. The vine leaves will probably burn a bit. Remove from grill, untie string and remove vine leaves (they can be served as a garnish, if desired). Cut salmon into four portions and serve with warm verjus butter.

SKATE WITH BLACK PEPPER AND SAUCE VIERGE

SERVES 2

Skate is a versatile fish that grills, fries and poaches well. It is still inexpensive — most people don't buy it because they are not sure how to cook it. Here's one way.

¼ cup olive oil	2 tbsp cracked peppercorns
1 tbsp lemon juice	1 lb skate wings
1 tsp cracked coriander seeds	Salt to taste
¼ cup chopped fresh coriander or basil	2 tbsp butter
2 tomatoes, seeded and chopped	• • • • •

Heat 2 tbsp olive oil in skillet on medium-low heat. Add lemon juice and coriander seeds and cook for about 2 minutes or until seeds are fragrant.

Remove from heat and add chopped coriander and tomatoes. Keep warm.

Pat peppercorns onto skate wings. Season with salt.

Heat remaining 2 tbsp oil in large skillet (or two, depending on size of wings) on medium heat. Add wings and cook for about 5 minutes or until golden. Add the butter to skillet, turn wings and cook until second side is golden. This should take 8 to 12 minutes in total, depending on size of wings.

Remove to serving plates and top with warm sauce.

SKATE

The kite-shaped skate lives near the ocean bottom. It is a mild fish with a taste similar to scallops, but only the wings are eaten. The wings are made up of flesh and cartilage that softens during cooking. Slide the flesh from the cartilage before serving or leave the wings whole.

POACHED SWORDFISH WITH COD BRANDADE

Pino Posteraro cooked sublime food in Italy and Toronto before going off to Vancouver. Several years ago he opened his own upscale restaurant there, Cioppino, a hit from day one. He cooks classic Mediterranean dishes reinvented with his own style and flair. The Poached Swordfish with Cod Brandade is a real winner, a recipe from his mother, he says, and what is simpler than that?

4 6-oz swordfish fillets

Salt and freshly ground pepper

2 cups fish stock

2 tbsp white wine

2 tbsp lemon juice

1 tbsp olive oil

24 mixed black and green olives

2 cloves garlic, very thinly sliced

1/4 cup Italian Parmesan cheese

2 tbsp chopped Italian parsley

• • • • •

GARNISH

Extra-virgin olive oil

Chervil sprigs

Preheat oven to 500 F. Season fish with salt and pepper. Place in a metal baking dish or skillet with a tight fitting lid. Pour over stock, wine, lemon juice, olive oil and olives.

Top each fillet with equal amounts of garlic, Parmesan and parsley. Cover and place in oven for 8-10 minutes or until slightly pink inside.

Place fish on serving plates, reserving cooking liquid and olives. Place liquid and olives in skillet. Reduce over high heat until slightly thickened, about 5 minutes.

Pour sauce over fish. Top with a sprinkle of extra-virgin olive oil and chervil sprigs. Serve with scoops of cod brandade.

FRESH COD BRANDADE

Brandade is usually made with salt cod, a quite involved process — using fresh cod makes this a very simple recipe.

Cook about 8 oz Yukon gold or baking potatoes. Drain and rice potatoes or beat until smooth. Meanwhile add 1/2 cup white wine, 2 tbsp lemon juice and 2 tbsp olive oil to a pot large enough to hold cod in one layer. Bring to boil, add cod, reduce heat to low, cover and cook until cod flakes easily, about 7 minutes. Remove cod and reduce liquid until 2 tbsp remain. Season. In a food processor combine potatoes, cod, reduced poaching liquid and 1/4 cup whipping cream. Puree. Taste for seasoning. Rewarm when needed. Serves 4.

GRILLED WHOLE SNAPPER WITH SICILIAN VINAIGRETTE

SERVES 4

Substitute striped bass or other whole fish if you wish. You can remove the heads before cooking, but the fish will be moister if you leave them on.

4 small red snappers, about 1 lb each, or 2 2-lb snappers
1/2 cup olive oil
1 tsp finely chopped garlic
Fresh oregano stalks, with leaves if possible

· · · · ·

SICILIAN VINAIGRETTE
2 tbsp finely chopped fresh oregano
1 tsp finely chopped garlic
2 tbsp finely chopped roasted or grilled red pepper (page 17)
3 tbsp balsamic vinegar
1/2 tsp grated lemon rind
1/2 cup olive oil
Salt and freshly ground pepper to taste

Rinse fish and pat dry. Whisk together oil and garlic. Brush on fish, both on skin and in cavities. Stuff oregano stalks in cavities. Marinate for 1 hour at room temperature.

Combine chopped oregano, garlic, red pepper, vinegar and lemon rind for vinaigrette. Slowly whisk in oil and season with salt and pepper.

Preheat grill on medium-high. Brush grill with oil. Grill fish for about 6 to 7 minutes per side for smaller fish, 8 to 10 minutes for larger, until flesh is white and moist and just comes away from bone.

Place fish on platter and cut fillets off bone if the fish are big. Otherwise serve one whole fish per person. Place on serving plates and drizzle with vinaigrette.

LEMON SNAPPER

SERVES 4

You can use sole, catfish, or tilapia instead of red snapper for this simple dish, but snapper has a sweeter taste.

½ cup all-purpose flour	¼ cup butter
1 tsp grated lemon rind	4 thin slices lemon, cut in quarters
Salt and freshly ground pepper to taste	½ tsp granulated sugar
4 8-oz red snapper fillets	½ cup chopped chives
¼ cup vegetable oil	• • • • •

Combine flour, lemon rind, salt and pepper on flat plate. Dredge fish with seasoned flour.

Add just enough oil in skillet to film base (you may not need the full ¼ cup). Heat oil on medium heat. Cook fish for 2 to 3 minutes per side or until golden. Remove to platter and keep warm.

Wipe out skillet, add butter and cook lemon pieces for 2 minutes. Sprinkle in sugar and continue to cook until lemon pieces are golden, about 2 to 3 minutes. Serve fish garnished with lemon and chives.

SEARED PEPPERED TUNA BURGERS WITH WASABI MAYONNAISE

SERVES 4

Buy frozen tuna, an inexpensive grade of fresh tuna or ask the fishmonger to give you ends and mince them in the food processor. Serve the burgers on sesame buns.

1 lb coarsely ground tuna	WASABI MAYONNAISE
2 tbsp soy sauce	2 tsp wasabi powder
2 tsp grated ginger	1/2 cup mayonnaise
1 tsp cracked peppercorns	1 tbsp soy sauce
1 tbsp cracked coriander seeds	1/2 tsp sesame oil
1 tbsp vegetable oil	• • • • •

Combine tuna, soy sauce and ginger. Gently form into 4 patties about 1 inch thick.

Combine peppercorns and coriander seeds and dust both sides of burgers with mixture.

Heat oil in skillet on medium-high heat. Cook burgers for 2 minutes per side or until medium-rare.

Combine wasabi powder, mayonnaise, soy sauce and sesame oil. Top burgers with wasabi mayonnaise.

FLASH-FRIED SQUID WITH TOMATO MINT SAUCE

SERVES 4

This is a special dish but the squid must be cooked very briefly or it becomes tough and rubbery. The textured sauce is excellent with all kinds of fish and chicken.

1 lb squid	2 cups chicken stock or water
Salt and freshly ground pepper to taste	1 tbsp lime juice
2 tbsp vegetable oil	¼ cup chopped fresh mint or Thai basil
1 tsp chopped garlic	• • • • •
1 tsp grated ginger	GARNISH
1 tsp red Thai curry paste	2 tsp chopped fresh mint or Thai basil
3 tbsp tomato paste	• • • • •

Slice squid into ¼-inch rings. Season with salt and pepper.

Heat 1 tbsp oil in skillet on medium heat. Stir in garlic, ginger and curry paste and sauté for 1 minute.

Stir in tomato paste and stock. Bring to boil, reduce heat and simmer for 5 minutes. Stir in lime juice and mint. Simmer for 2 minutes or until sauce thickens slightly. Strain sauce into measuring cup.

Wipe out pan, place on high heat and add remaining 1 tbsp oil. Add squid and sauté for 1 minute or until opaque. Pour in strained sauce, bring to boil and serve immediately. Garnish with chopped mint.

CARAMELIZED SHRIMP

SERVES 4

A dynamite dish of large shrimp coated with a salty-sweet caramel sauce. Serve with rice.

½ cup brown sugar	2 tsp chopped garlic
3 tbsp soy sauce	½ small onion, sliced
¼ cup water	12 oz large shrimp, shelled
¼ cup rice vinegar	1 tsp grated lime rind
2 tsp grated ginger	¼ tsp Asian chili sauce
1 tbsp vegetable oil	3 green onions, cut in 1-inch pieces

Combine sugar, soy sauce, water, vinegar and ginger in small pot. Bring to boil on high heat and boil until sauce thickens and forms a soft drip off end of cold spoon, about 4 minutes. Remove from heat and reserve.

Heat oil in wok on high heat. Add garlic and onion and stir-fry until onion is tinged with gold, about 3 minutes.

Add shrimp and stir-fry for 1 minute. Add reserved sauce, lime rind, chili sauce and green onions and cook for 1 minute until shrimp is pink and curled. Stir in a little extra if sauce is too thick.

GOAN SHRIMP

SERVES 4

Goa, where you can find some of the best food in India, has a reputation for very hot yet well-balanced food. It is the home of vindaloo, the fieriest of curries. This dish is not too hot but still exciting. Serve on skewers as an hors d'oeuvre or remove from skewers to serve as a main course with rice and Curried Green Beans (page 168).

1 tbsp white vinegar	YOGURT MINT SAUCE
1 tbsp grated ginger	½ cup mint chutney or mint sauce
1 tbsp chopped garlic	½ cup yogurt
1 tsp garam masala (page 5) or	• • • • •
Indian curry powder	GARNISH
¼ cup vegetable oil	Sliced onions
2 lb large shrimp, shelled	Sliced limes
• • • • •	Sliced cucumbers
	Sprigs fresh mint

Combine vinegar, ginger, garlic, garam masala and oil. Pour over shrimp and marinate at room temperature for 1 hour or refrigerate overnight.

Combine mint chutney and yogurt and reserve.

Skewer shrimp on bamboo skewers that have been soaked in water for 30 minutes. Make sure skewer goes through whole body of shrimp.

Grill on high heat for about 2 minutes per side or until shrimp are pink and firm.

Line platter with onions, limes and cucumbers. Place skewers on bed of vegetables. Garnish with fresh mint and serve with sauce.

BRINED SHRIMP

SERVES 6 AS AN APPETIZER

Most of our shrimp is frozen and defrosted, but brining restores the original flavor and tex-
ture. (You can use this brining method for any shrimp recipe.)
Serve the shrimp hot or cold with Roasted Garlic and Chili Pesto.

1/2 cup kosher salt	4 cups cold water
1 cup boiling water	2 lb large shrimp

Dissolve salt in boiling water. Stir in cold water. Cool.

Cut down back of shrimp through shells but do not remove shells. Add shrimp to brine and let sit for 45 minutes. Drain shrimp and rinse.

Grill shrimp on high heat for about 2 minutes per side or until pink and slightly curled.

ROASTED GARLIC AND CHILI PESTO

In food processor, combine 1 head roasted garlic, 1 grilled and seeded jalapeño pepper, 1 1/2 cups fresh coriander, 2 tbsp chopped almonds and 1 tbsp lemon juice. Process until chunky. With machine running, slowly add 1/2 cup olive oil through feed tube. Mixture will thicken.

Makes 1 1/2 to 2 cups.

ROASTING GARLIC

Cut off stalk ends, remove any flaky skin but do not peel. Separate into cloves and place in foil. Sprinkle with 2 tbsp olive oil and bake at 400 F for 30 to 40 minutes or until soft and golden coloured. Remove from skins by pressing from base of clove.

THAI SHRIMP AND VEGETABLE CURRY

SERVES 4

A simple, quick curry. Use the long, thin Asian eggplants; they are sweeter and more thin-skinned than the regular ones. Lime leaves look like bay leaves but have a floral aroma and flavor. They are available at Asian markets; freeze what you don't use for another time. Otherwise, substitute grated lime rind.

Serve this curry with Sticky Rice.

1 tbsp vegetable oil	1 14-oz (398 mL) can coconut milk
1 cup chopped onions	1 cup fish stock or chicken stock
1 tbsp grated ginger	2 lime leaves or 1 tbsp grated lime rind
1 tbsp chopped garlic	1 tbsp lime juice
1 tsp red Thai curry paste or more to taste	1 cup seeded and diced tomatoes
1 small Asian eggplant, cut in ½ inch slices	1 lb large shrimp, shelled
1 small zucchini, cut in ½-inch slices	¼ cup chopped fresh coriander or mint

Heat oil in large skillet or wok on medium-high heat. Add onions and stir-fry for 1 minute. Add ginger and garlic and stir-fry for 30 seconds. Add curry paste and stir-fry for 1 minute.

Add eggplant and zucchini and stir-fry until well combined, about 2 minutes.

Stir in coconut milk, stock and lime leaves. Bring to boil, reduce heat and simmer for 15 minutes or until vegetables are cooked.

Stir in lime juice, tomatoes and shrimp. Simmer for 5 minutes or until shrimp are pink and curled. Stir in coriander.

STICKY RICE

Sticky rice is a Thai staple. The opaque, long-grained rice becomes sticky when it is cooked, and its sweet taste goes beautifully with spicy food. It is also known as glutinous rice or sweet rice. Japanese sushi rice can be used as a substitute.

To cook sticky rice, soak in water for 1 to 2 hours. Rinse and place in steamer or sieve lined with clean cloth or Boston lettuce leaves. Place over pot or wok of boiling water, cover and steam for 20 to 25 minutes or until the rice is tender.

ORANGE-SCENTED SCALLOPS

This quick sauté can be served as a first course garnished with salad greens or as a main course with rice and asparagus.

1 lb large scallops	½ cup freshly squeezed orange juice
Salt and freshly ground pepper to taste	2 tbsp chopped fresh dill
2 tbsp olive oil	2 tbsp butter

Remove side muscles from scallops (they attach the scallop to the shell and can be tough). Season scallops with salt and pepper.

Heat oil in skillet on medium-high heat. Add scallops and sear for 2 minutes on each side or just until opaque.

Remove scallops from skillet and reduce heat to low. Add orange juice and dill. Bring to boil, whisk in butter and pour over scallops.

GRILLED MUSSELS AND CLAMS

SERVES 6 AS A FIRST COURSE

A fabulous first course that can be cooked quickly on the barbecue. Remove the clams and mussels from the grill as soon as they open. Serve with Wasabi Sauce and garnish with lemon wedges or use as a topping for linguine tossed with tomato sauce.

1 lb mussels   1 1/2 lb clams

Wash mussels and clams and place on grill. Cover and grill until shells open, about 2 to 3 minutes for mussels and 5 to 7 minutes for clams.

WASABI SAUCE

Combine 2 tbsp wasabi powder with 2 tbsp water. Stir wasabi mixture into 1/2 cup yogurt. Beat in 1/2 cup mayonnaise, 2 tbsp chopped pickled ginger, 2 tbsp lemon juice, and salt and freshly ground pepper to taste.

Makes about 1 1/2 cups.

OYSTER GRATIN

Buy shucked oysters for this heady dish. If you are using the large B.C. oysters, cut them in half.

This makes a perfect first course for a romantic dinner, but the recipe doubles beautifully if you want to serve it as a main course. For an elegant presentation, serve in oyster shells.

¼ cup butter	½ cup chopped watercress
2 tbsp chopped parsley	3 tbsp dry breadcrumbs
2 tbsp chopped celery	1 tsp Pernod or anisette, optional
2 green onions, chopped	Salt and freshly ground pepper to taste
½ tsp chopped garlic	8 oysters

Preheat oven to 400 F.

Melt butter in skillet on medium-high heat. When butter sizzles, add parsley, celery, green onions and garlic. Cook for 3 minutes. Add watercress and cook for 1 minute.

Place mixture in food processor and puree with 2 tbsp breadcrumbs and Pernod. Season with salt and pepper.

Place oysters and any juice in small gratin dish. Top with watercress puree and sprinkle with remaining 1 tbsp breadcrumbs.

Bake for 5 to 7 minutes or until edges of oysters curl slightly.

CHAPTER 5

Poultry

It is also a waste of good food to serve it to new lovers.
– M.F.K. Fisher

MEXICAN CHICKEN WITH GRILLED TOMATO AVOCADO SALSA

SERVES 4

This slightly spicy, citrus-scented chicken should be served with warm tortillas. You can substitute boneless skinless chicken breasts, but they will take 2 minutes less grilling time. Grilling the vegetables gives the salsa a depth of flavor that heightens the whole dish.

2 large tomatoes	3 tbsp olive oil
1 small red onion	Salt to taste
2 jalapeño peppers	4 boneless single chicken breasts, with skin
3 cloves garlic, unpeeled	1 avocado, peeled
2 tbsp orange juice	2 tbsp chopped fresh coriander
1 tbsp lemon juice	• • • • •

Cut tomatoes and red onion into slices ½ inch thick. Cut jalapeños in half and remove seeds.

Place tomatoes, onion, jalapeños and garlic cloves in grill basket or directly on grill and grill for about 2 minutes on each side, with lid down, until vegetables are charred and garlic skin comes off. Remove from grill, cool and chop. Stir in orange juice, lemon juice and 2 tbsp olive oil. Season with salt.

Chop ½ cup tomato mixture finely. Spread 2 tbsp finely chopped mixture under skin of each chicken breast.

Brush chicken with remaining 1 tbsp olive oil. Grill for 5 minutes per side or until juices are clear.

Chop avocado while chicken is cooking and stir into remaining tomato mixture. Stir in coriander.

Slice chicken into ½-inch slices and serve with salsa.

HERB-ROASTED CHICKEN WITH ZUCCHINI AND RED ONIONS

SERVES 4

Use tarragon, parsley, basil, rosemary, or a combination in this recipe. Serve with rice or couscous.

2 green or yellow zucchini

2 small red onions, peeled

10 fresh sage leaves, torn in thirds

2 tbsp olive oil

Salt and freshly ground pepper to taste

2 tbsp chopped fresh herbs

2 tbsp butter, at room temperature

4 boneless single chicken breasts, with skin

Preheat oven to 425 F.

Cut zucchini into slices 1 inch thick. Cut onions into quarters. Combine zucchini and onions in roasting pan. Toss with sage, oil, salt and pepper.

Bake for 25 minutes.

Combine herbs and butter in food processor or by hand. Season with salt and pepper. Spread butter underneath chicken skin and on top.

Heat non-stick skillet on medium-high heat. Add chicken skin side down. Cook for 3 minutes or until skin browns. Cook second side for 3 minutes.

Place chicken on top of vegetables and pour over any butter from pan. Bake for 10 to 15 minutes or until vegetables are tender and chicken is cooked.

Serve chicken and vegetables along with any pan juices.

ASIAN ROAST CHICKEN

SERVES 4

Although the lemon grass gives this dish a Thai flavor, you can also substitute grated lemon or lime rind. Serve with rice noodles tossed with sesame oil and green onions.

2 stalks lemon grass	1 tbsp vegetable oil
1 tbsp grated ginger	Asian chili sauce to taste, optional
1 tbsp finely chopped garlic	1 3-lb chicken, butterflied
3 tbsp finely chopped fresh coriander or mint	Salt to taste
1 tbsp soy sauce	• • • • •

Strip hard outer leaves from lemon grass and discard. Chop tender part of bulb finely (you should have about 2 tbsp).

Combine lemon grass, ginger, garlic, coriander, soy sauce, oil and chili sauce. Spread over chicken on both sides, spreading a little under skin, if possible. Marinate for 1 hour at room temperature. Salt chicken.

Preheat oven to 400 F.

Place chicken on rack in roasting pan and roast for 45 to 60 minutes or until juices are clear. Cut into 4 pieces and serve.

BUTTERFLYING CHICKEN

Cutting out the backbone and flattening the chicken allows quick cooking and easy carving. The butcher will remove the backbone for you; failing that, cut down either side of the backbone with kitchen shears. Remove bone and discard or use for stock. Turn chicken and remove breastbone to allow chicken to lie flat and cook more evenly.

ITALIAN ROAST CHICKEN

Marinate chicken in 1/2 cup pesto (page 60) and 2 tbsp olive oil.

INDIAN ROAST CHICKEN

Marinate chicken in 1/2 cup yogurt, 1 tbsp Indian curry paste, pinch saffron and 1 tbsp lime juice.

FRENCH ROAST CHICKEN

Marinate chicken in 1 tbsp chopped fresh tarragon, 2 tbsp olive oil and 1 tsp chopped garlic.

CRISP-SKINNED ROAST CHICKEN

Serves 4

Heavily salting and peppering the chicken skin before roasting means you will have the crispiest chicken ever. The skin becomes very crisp because the salt draws out the moisture. Buy a whole chicken that is air chilled and preferably free range. They have more flavour.

1 4-lb chicken	SAUCE
2 tsp kosher salt	1 tbsp soy sauce
Freshly ground pepper to taste	1 cup chicken stock
2 tbsp melted butter	1 tsp lemon juice
· · · · ·	1 tbsp cornstarch mixed with 1 tbsp water

Preheat oven to 400 F.

Season chicken in cavity and on skin with salt and pepper. Drizzle skin with melted butter. Place on rack in roasting pan. Roast 1 hour and 15 minutes or until juices are clear. Place on carving board and let rest for 10 minutes.

Skim fat from roasting pan. Place on high heat and stir in soy sauce, chicken stock and lemon juice. Bring to boil and slowly stir in enough cornstarch mixture to thicken a little. Season well. Carve chicken and serve with sauce.

STUFFED CHICKEN MEATLOAF

SERVES 8

This recipe is a meatloaf in name only. It presents beautifully with an outside layer of chicken and a heart of green and white. Serve with roasted sweet potatoes. The chicken and filling can also be layered and baked in a loaf pan.

2 lb ground chicken	3 leeks, trimmed and chopped
Salt and freshly ground pepper to taste	4 cups baby spinach
1 tbsp butter	1 tbsp chopped garlic
1 cup finely chopped onions	1 tbsp lemon juice
2 eggs	1/2 cup ricotta cheese
2 tsp Worcestershire sauce	1 egg, beaten
1 tsp dried tarragon	1/4 cup dry breadcrumbs
2 tbsp chopped parsley	1/2 cup grated Parmesan cheese
1 cup dry breadcrumbs	• • • • •
• • • • •	GLAZE
FILLING	2 tbsp soy sauce
1/2 cup chicken stock or water	1 tsp maple syrup

Preheat oven to 350 F.

Season chicken with salt and pepper.

Heat butter in skillet on medium heat. Add onions and sauté until limp, about 2 minutes. Add to chicken.

Combine eggs, Worcestershire, tarragon, parsley, salt and pepper. Add to chicken with breadcrumbs. Cook small portion of chicken in skillet to test for seasoning. Add salt and pepper if necessary.

Heat chicken stock in skillet until simmering. Add leeks, spinach and garlic and simmer, covered, until leeks are soft, about 5 minutes. Drain very well.

Place leeks, spinach and garlic in food processor

with lemon juice, ricotta, beaten egg and breadcrumbs. Combine until slightly chunky. Stir in Parmesan, salt and pepper.

Spread chicken on large sheet of waxed paper to form rectangle 1/2 inch thick. Spread leek and spinach filling over chicken, leaving 1/2-inch border all the way around.

Roll chicken around filling using waxed paper as a guide. Flip rolled chicken onto baking sheet, seam side down.

Combine soy sauce and maple syrup. Brush chicken with mixture.

Bake for 45 minutes or until juices rise and are clear. Cool slightly and cut into slices.

VIETNAMESE CHICKEN

SERVES 4

Chicken thighs are juicier than breasts and can be found boned and skinned at many super-markets. You can grill the chicken instead of baking it, if desired.
Serve with Vietnamese Dipping Sauce and rice noodles, drizzled with extra dipping sauce.

12 boneless, skinless chicken thighs or 4 boneless,
skinless single chicken breasts
2 green onions, finely chopped
1 tsp grated lemon rind
1 tbsp finely chopped garlic
1 tbsp granulated sugar

2 tbsp chopped fresh mint
2 tbsp chopped fresh coriander
2 tbsp Thai fish sauce
1 tbsp lemon juice
3 tbsp vegetable oil
• • • • •

Trim chicken thighs of all fat.

Combine green onions, lemon rind, garlic, sugar, mint, coriander, fish sauce, lemon juice and 2 tbsp vegetable oil. Toss with chicken thighs. Marinate for 1 hour at room temperature or refrigerate overnight. Turn chicken occasionally. Remove chicken from marinade.

Preheat oven to 400 F.

Heat remaining 1 tbsp oil in skillet on medium heat. Add thighs and brown for about 2 to 3 minutes per side. (Dish may be prepared a few hours ahead to this point.)

Place chicken on baking sheet and bake for 15 to 20 minutes or until juices are clear.

VIETNAMESE DIPPING SAUCE

The red pepper adds color but it can be omitted. The sauce will keep for at least two weeks in the refrigerator.

Combine 1/4 cup water and 1 cup granulated sugar in pot. Bring to boil and boil for 5 minutes or until slightly syrupy. Cool.

In a food processor puree 1/2 red pepper, 2 cloves garlic, 1/4 cup Thai fish sauce, 1/4 cup lime juice and 1/4 cup sugar syrup. Add more syrup if sauce is too thick. Pour sauce into bowl and garnish with grated carrots.

Makes about 1 cup. Extra syrup keeps refrigerated for a month.

MOROCCAN-STYLE POACHED CHICKEN

SERVES 4

Although the ingredient list looks long, this is a very simple but highly flavorful one-pot meal.
Serve it with storebought or homemade harissa (page 6) or with Asian chili sauce.

2 tbsp olive oil	Pinch saffron threads, crushed
1 onion, chopped	Salt and freshly ground pepper to taste
1/2 cup chopped carrots	1 1/2 lb boneless, skinless chicken breasts,
2 tsp chopped garlic	cut in 2-inch pieces
1/2 tsp ground cumin	1 zucchini, cut in 1/2-inch dice
1/2 tsp dried ground ginger	1 portobello mushroom, trimmed and
1 tsp paprika	cut in 1/2-inch dice
1/2 tsp cayenne	1 1/2 cups couscous
2 tsp tomato paste	2 tbsp chopped fresh coriander
1 cup chopped tomatoes	1 lemon, cut in wedges
2 cups chicken stock or water	. . . . .

Heat oil in large skillet on medium-high heat. Add onion, carrots and garlic and sauté for 3 minutes or until softened. Add cumin, ginger, paprika and cayenne and sauté for 1 minute.

Stir in tomato paste, tomatoes, stock and saffron. Bring to boil, reduce heat and simmer for 8 to 10 minutes or until sauce thickens slightly. Season with salt and pepper.

Reduce heat to medium-low. Add chicken, zucchini and mushrooms to sauce. Poach for 5 to 7 minutes, turning chicken pieces to cook evenly. Chicken should be just cooked.

Pour 1 1/2 cups chicken cooking liquid over couscous in bowl, adding boiling water if necessary. Cover and let sit for 5 minutes. Fluff up and stir into chicken and vegetable mixture. Sprinkle with coriander and garnish with lemon.

SOY SAUCE POACHED CHICKEN BREASTS

SERVES 4

A refreshing summer dish that can be served with Asian slaw and rice or noodles. The chicken is also good sliced and served on pita or dried apple slices as an hors d'oeuvre.

1 cup soy sauce	3 thin slices ginger
1/2 cup water	1 tsp cinnamon
1/4 cup white wine	1/2 tsp grated nutmeg
1/2 cup granulated sugar	4 boneless, skinless single chicken breasts

Bring soy sauce, water, wine, sugar, ginger, cinnamon and nutmeg to boil in large skillet over high heat. Reduce heat to simmer.

Add chicken breasts and simmer for 8 minutes on each side or until chicken is just tinged with pink in center. Remove from heat and cool in liquid.

Slice chicken and serve.

ASIAN SLAW

This keeps for about 4 days in the refrigerator. Add leftover shredded chicken or turkey to the salad for a casual meal.

To make the dressing, combine 2 tbsp lime juice, 1/2 cup rice vinegar, 1/2 tsp Asian chili sauce (or more to taste), 2 tsp finely chopped garlic, 2 tbsp Thai fish sauce, 2 tbsp vegetable oil and 2 tsp sesame oil.

Combine 4 cups shredded green cabbage, 1 cup grated carrots and 1/2 cup chopped green onions. Toss with dressing and garnish with black or white sesame seeds. Season with salt and freshly ground pepper to taste.

Makes 4 cups.

CHICKEN BREASTS WITH MANY HERB LEAVES

SERVES 4

Roasted chicken breasts perfumed with herbs make a winning fall dish when herbs are over-running your garden. Serve with Saffron Aioli.

2 tbsp olive oil

20 fresh sage leaves

20 fresh basil leaves

20 fresh mint leaves

4 boneless single chicken breasts, with skin

Salt and freshly ground pepper to taste

2 tbsp lemon juice

• • • • •

Preheat oven to 400 F.

Heat oil in large ovenproof skillet on medium heat. Add sage, basil and mint leaves and sauté until translucent, about 2 minutes. Remove from skillet and reserve.

Place chicken skin side down in skillet and sauté until skin is golden, about 3 minutes. Turn and cook second side for 2 minutes. Scatter fried herbs over chicken and season with salt and pepper.

Place skillet in oven and bake chicken for 15 minutes or until juices run clear. Remove and sprinkle with lemon juice.

SAFFRON AIOLI

Soak ½ tsp crushed saffron threads in 2 tbsp boiling water for 5 minutes. Whisk in 1 tsp finely chopped garlic and ½ cup mayonnaise. Season with salt, freshly ground pepper and lemon juice to taste. Thin with extra warm water if necessary.

Makes about ½ cup.

CRISP BUTTERMILK FRIED CHICKEN

SERVES 4

This can be served hot or cold. Panko breadcrumbs will give you a very crisp coating, but you can also use regular breadcrumbs. Serve with chutney or Ginger Peach Relish.

1 cup buttermilk	2 tsp dried thyme
1 3-lb chicken, cut in serving pieces	1 tbsp coarsely ground pepper
Salt and freshly ground pepper to taste	Pinch cayenne
2 cups panko or fresh breadcrumbs	Salt to taste
1 tbsp paprika	¼ cup vegetable oil

Pour buttermilk over chicken pieces and marinate for 1 hour at room temperature or refrigerate overnight. Drain. Season chicken with salt and pepper.

Preheat oven to 400 F.

Combine panko, paprika, thyme, pepper, cayenne and salt in plastic bag. Add chicken and shake in mixture until chicken is lightly coated. Shake off any excess.

Heat oil in large skillet on medium-high heat. Add chicken pieces a few at a time (do not crowd pan) and fry on each side until golden, about 2 to 3 minutes per side.

Place chicken on baking sheet and bake for 20 to 25 minutes or until juices are clear.

GINGER PEACH RELISH

Extra relish will keep for up to 1 month in the refrigerator.

Combine 2 tbsp grated ginger, ½ cup peach or mango nectar, ¼ cup lime juice, 1 tsp hot red pepper sauce and ¼ cup chopped fresh mint in pot on medium heat. Bring to boil and reduce heat. Add 4 cups peeled and chopped peaches and simmer for 10 minutes or until peaches are tender. Cool and stir in another ¼ cup chopped fresh mint.

Makes about 4 cups.

PANKO

These Japanese breadcrumbs are large, coarse and light, and they give food a crunchier coating than regular breadcrumbs. You can find them in the Asian food section of supermarkets or in Asian grocery stores.

MALAYSIAN CHICKEN AND RICE

SERVES 3 TO 4

This is one of the great dishes from Singapore — flavorful, low-fat and satisfying. Make the stock from good-quality bouillon cubes or buy the chicken broth sold in Tetrapaks.

Except for the rice, this can all be made ahead of time. Serve the chicken, rice and soup with one or two dipping sauces.

4 slices ginger, smashed	1 tbsp chopped garlic
2 green onions	2 cups uncooked long-grain rice (preferably Thai
1 3-lb chicken	jasmine), rinsed
6 to 8 cups chicken stock	Salt to taste
1 tsp sesame oil	1/2 English cucumber, thinly sliced
1 tbsp vegetable oil	1 tomato, sliced
1 tbsp grated ginger	• • • • •

Place ginger slices and green onions in cavity of chicken.

Bring stock to boil in large pot and immerse chicken in stock. Chicken should be covered in stock. Return to boil, reduce heat to low, cover and poach chicken for 30 to 40 minutes or until juices are clear.

Remove chicken from stock and immediately immerse in ice water to stop the cooking. (This is an important step to make sure chicken stays juicy.) Reserve 2 1/2 cups stock. Skim fat from remaining stock and keep hot to serve as soup.

Cool chicken, then remove from ice water and drain well. Take chicken off bones and brush with sesame oil (remove skin, if desired). Cut chicken into small pieces.

Heat vegetable oil in heavy pot. Add grated ginger and garlic and sauté for 2 minutes or until fragrant. Add rice and sauté for 1 minute.

Pour in reserved 2 1/2 cups stock and bring to boil. Let boil for 2 minutes, reduce heat to low, cover and steam rice for 20 minutes. Stir rice and add salt if necessary.

Place chicken on platter, surround with cucumber and tomato slices and serve with rice and soup.

SOY SESAME DIPPING SAUCE

Combine 3 tbsp soy and 1 tbsp sesame oil.

Makes 1/4 cup.

CHILI GINGER SAUCE

Combine 1 tbsp grated ginger, 2 tsp finely chopped garlic and 1 tsp Asian chili sauce. Stir in 1/4 cup chicken stock, 1 tbsp soy sauce, 1 tsp sesame oil, 1 tbsp rice vinegar and 1 tsp granulated sugar.

Makes about 1/3 cup.

CHICKEN "SANDWICH"

SERVES 2 TO 3

This wonderful dish is based on an idea from my mother, Pearl Geneen. It can be served hot with gravy, mashed potatoes and a salad for a light dinner. For the best texture, grind your own chicken (it is easier to chop/grind the meat if it is partially frozen). Chicken breasts can also be used (reduce the baking time by 5 minutes), but they are not as juicy. Use an inexpensive white bread in this recipe, as it flattens out easily.

1 lb boneless, skinless chicken thighs, cut in chunks	2 tbsp dry breadcrumbs
1 egg white	½ cup chopped watercress
½ cup chopped onions	Salt and freshly ground pepper to taste
1 tsp finely chopped garlic	4 slices white sandwich bread
1 tsp chopped fresh rosemary or ¼ tsp dried	2 tbsp olive oil
	1 egg, beaten

Preheat oven to 400 F.

Chop chicken coarsely in food processor or by hand (leave some texture).

Combine chicken, egg white, onions, garlic, rosemary, breadcrumbs and watercress. Season with salt and pepper.

Roll out bread slices with rolling pin until very thin. Brush both sides of bread with oil. Dip bread slices in beaten egg.

Place two slices bread on oiled, foil-lined baking sheet. Divide chicken mixture between them and spread to edge of bread. Top with remaining two slices. Press down with spatula (sandwiches will still be quite thick).

Bake for 20 to 25 minutes, turning once, until white juices start to appear. Bread should be crisp and golden on both sides. Cool on rack or serve warm. Slice into pieces before serving.

MANDARIN CHICKEN ROLLS

SERVES 4

Letting guests make their own rolls is a good way to break the ice at a dinner party. Serve as a main course for a casual dinner with a noodle soup first.

2 tbsp soy sauce	8 small flour tortillas
1 tbsp honey	½ cup hoisin sauce
4 boneless single chicken breasts, with skin	1 seedless cucumber, peeled and cut in 3-inch strips
Freshly ground pepper to taste	
1 tbsp vegetable oil	6 green onions, cut in 3-inch lengths

Combine soy sauce and honey.

Slash skin of each chicken breast in 4 places. Brush chicken with soy sauce/honey mixture. Season well with pepper. Marinate for 30 minutes at room temperature.

Preheat oven to 400 F.

Heat oil in ovenproof skillet on medium-high heat. Add chicken, skin side down, and cook for 2 minutes or until colored. Turn chicken and cook for 2 minutes. Turn skin side down again.

Place skillet in oven and bake for 8 to 10 minutes or until juices run clear. Remove from oven and let chicken rest on carving board for 5 minutes.

Wrap tortillas in foil. Bake for 5 minutes or until warm.

Cut chicken into thin slices. Let guests assemble their own rolls by spreading hoisin on tortillas and rolling up chicken, cucumber and onions.

QUICK LEMON CHICKEN

SERVES 4

Good-quality free range chicken breasts require little embellishment beyond fresh lemon and herbs. The lemon slices can be brushed with a little olive oil and grilled alongside the chicken.

Serve with Barley Risotto with Spinach (page 149).

1 tsp grated lemon rind	4 boneless, skinless single chicken breasts
2 tbsp lemon juice	Salt and freshly ground pepper to taste
2 tbsp olive oil	4 slices lemon
2 tsp chopped fresh tarragon or 1/2 tsp dried	• • • • •

Combine lemon rind and juice, oil, tarragon, salt and pepper. Brush over chicken and marinate for 10 minutes.

Grill chicken for 5 to 8 minutes per side or until juice is no longer pink. Serve with lemon slices.

CHICKEN UNDER A BRICK

SERVES 4

In this recipe, the pressure of the weight makes the skin crisp and helps the seasonings permeate the flesh. The chicken also cooks more quickly and more evenly. Use two double breasts if you can find them. Serve on a lettuce-lined platter garnished with onion rings and sliced radishes, along with Garlic Walnut Sauce.

2 boneless double chicken breasts, skin on

1 tbsp chopped fresh rosemary or 1 tsp dried

1 tbsp chopped fresh tarragon or 1 tsp dried

1 tsp finely chopped garlic

Salt and freshly ground pepper to taste

2 tbsp olive oil

1 tbsp butter

. . . . .

Place chicken between 2 sheets of plastic wrap or parchment paper. Pound with a heavy skillet to flatten to an even thickness. Remove paper.

Combine rosemary, tarragon, garlic, salt and pepper. Rub seasonings over chicken.

Heat oil and butter in large heavy skillet on medium-high heat. Add chicken skin side down and cook for 2 minutes. (You may have to cook the breasts in 2 skillets.) Reduce heat to medium-low.

Place parchment paper over chicken and place heavy skillet or pot on paper. Place cans on skillet for more weight.

Cook chicken for 7 minutes or until skin is golden and crispy. Remove weights and turn chicken. Replace parchment, skillet and weights and cook for 5 minutes or until chicken is cooked though. Cut chicken into slices.

GARLIC WALNUT SAUCE

Combine in food processor 1 cup chopped toasted walnuts, 1 tbsp chopped garlic, 1/2 cup chopped fresh coriander, 1/2 tsp dried ground coriander, pinch cayenne, 2 tbsp olive oil, 1/2 cup chicken stock and 2 tbsp lemon juice. Process until chunky. The mixture should have some texture. Season with salt and freshly ground pepper to taste and more lemon juice if necessary.

Makes about 1 cup.

PERUVIAN CHICKEN

SERVES 4

A spicy, herbal, oven-fried chicken to serve with rice, Avocado Salad and Pineapple Salsa. Brown the chicken ahead of time and bake before serving. You can use breasts instead of thighs in this recipe, but reduce the cooking time by a few minutes.
This dish should be made with fresh herbs.

12 chicken thighs or legs, bone-in (about 3 lb)	½ tsp chopped garlic
Grated rind and juice of 1 lime	1 tsp chopped jalapeño pepper
2 tbsp chopped fresh thyme	1 cup all-purpose flour
2 tbsp chopped fresh basil	Salt and freshly ground pepper to taste
2 tbsp chopped fresh sage	2 tbsp olive oil

Trim fat from thighs.

Combine lime rind and juice, thyme, basil, sage, garlic and jalapeño. Toss with chicken and marinate for 30 minutes at room temperature.

Preheat oven to 400 F.

Combine flour, salt and pepper. Lightly dredge thighs in seasoned flour.

Heat oil in non-stick skillet on medium heat. Add chicken pieces skin side down and cook for 3 minutes per side or until golden. Place on baking sheet.

Bake chicken for 20 to 25 minutes or until juices are clear.

PINEAPPLE SALSA

Brush 4 rings fresh pineapple with oil. Grill or cook in non-stick pan on both sides until golden. Cool and dice. Combine pineapple with ½ cup chopped red onion, ½ cup chopped red pepper, ¼ cup lime juice, 2 tbsp pineapple juice, 3 tbsp chopped fresh mint and 1 tbsp granulated sugar. Season with salt and freshly ground pepper to taste.

Makes about 2 cups.

AVOCADO SALAD

Combine ¼ cup fresh lime juice with ¼ cup olive oil and season with salt and freshly ground pepper to taste. Peel and dice 2 large avocados and combine with ¼ cup chopped red onion. Toss with lime dressing and sprinkle with chopped fresh coriander to taste.

Serves 4.

SAUTÉED CHICKEN WITH APPLES AND CREAM

SERVES 4

A quick sauté to serve with Mediterranean Roasted Potatoes (page 173) and a watercress salad. Use Calvados, an apple-flavored brandy, or regular brandy.

4 boneless, skinless single chicken breasts	1 tsp chopped fresh thyme or pinch dried
Salt and freshly ground pepper to taste	1/2 cup white wine
1/4 cup butter	1/2 cup whipping cream
2 green apples, peeled and sliced	2 tbsp Calvados, optional

Season chicken with salt and pepper.

Heat 2 tbsp butter in skillet on medium heat. Add apples and thyme and sauté until apples soften, about 5 minutes. Remove apples and add remaining 2 tbsp butter to skillet.

Add chicken breasts and sauté for 3 to 4 minutes on each side or until golden. Pour in wine, bring to boil and reduce until 2 tbsp remains.

Add cream and Calvados. Return apples to skillet and simmer for 2 minutes or just until sauce thickens and chicken juices run clear.

DUCK BREASTS WITH BLOOD ORANGE SAUCE

SERVES 4

Slowly cooking the duck breasts skin side down releases the fat and crisps the skin. Finish with a fast oven bake. Serve the duck with Oven-roasted Potatoes and Turnips.
If blood oranges are unavailable (they add a beautiful color), use regular oranges.

2 duck breasts, about 1 lb each	2 tbsp balsamic vinegar
Salt and freshly ground pepper to taste	2 cups chicken stock
1/2 cup blood orange juice	1 tbsp butter
1/2 cup red wine	. . . . .

Preheat oven to 450 F.

Score top of duck breasts. Season with salt and pepper. Place in cold ovenproof skillet skin side down and place on medium heat. Cook for 2 minutes.

Reduce heat to low and cook duck for 15 minutes or until fat is rendered and skin begins to crisp. Pour out fat and turn duck.

Place skillet in oven and bake for 10 to 12 minutes or until duck is medium- rare. Remove from skillet and let rest for 5 minutes.

Pour any fat from skillet. Add orange juice, wine and vinegar to skillet and place on high heat. Bring to boil and cook for about 5 minutes or until reduced by half. Stir in stock and boil until sauce thickens slightly, about 3 to 5 minutes. Remove from heat and whisk in butter. Season with salt and pepper.

Carve duck into 1/2-inch slices and drizzle with sauce.

OVEN-ROASTED POTATOES AND TURNIPS

Bring large pot water to boil. Add 3 cups peeled, diced rutabaga, return to boil and boil for 7 minutes. Add 3 cups peeled, diced potatoes to pot and boil for 5 minutes longer. Drain well, season with salt and pepper and toss with 2 tbsp duck fat or olive oil and a sprinkle of dried rosemary. Place in baking dish and roast at 450 F for 20 minutes or until golden, tossing occasionally.

Serves 4.

ROASTED TURKEY BREAST WITH SAVORY GARLIC SAUCE

Turkey breasts can be purchased rolled and tied or as single or double breasts. If you end up with two smaller breasts, just bake them side by side.

¼ cup butter, at room temperature	2 cups sliced onions
1 tsp finely chopped garlic	1 cup sliced carrots
1 tbsp finely chopped fresh tarragon or 1 tsp dried	6 cloves garlic, peeled
Salt and freshly ground pepper to taste	½ cup white wine
1 tsp grated lemon rind	3 cups chicken stock or turkey stock
1 tbsp lemon juice	1 tbsp balsamic vinegar
1 4-lb boneless turkey breast, with skin	1 tbsp soy sauce
1 tbsp Dijon mustard	. . . . .

Preheat oven to 400 F.

Cream together butter, chopped garlic, tarragon, salt, pepper, lemon rind and juice. Reserve 1 tbsp. With fingertips, gently ease turkey skin away from breast, forming a cavity. Stuff remaining garlic butter under skin and in any cavities in turkey breast.

Melt reserved 1 tbsp seasoned butter and combine with mustard. Spread over top and underside of turkey. Season breast well with salt and pepper.

Sprinkle onions, carrots and whole garlic cloves over bottom of roasting pan. Pour wine over vegetables. Place turkey breast on top.

Roast for 1¼ to 1½ hours or until juices run clear. Let turkey rest for 10 minutes while making sauce.

Skim fat from roasting pan and add contents of pan to food processor or blender. Puree until smooth. Return to roasting pan with chicken stock. Whisk in tomato paste, vinegar and soy sauce. Bring to boil, reduce heat and simmer for 5 minutes. Taste for seasoning, adding salt or pepper if necessary.

Carve turkey and serve with sauce.

SPICED CORNISH HENS

SERVES 4

To crush the spice mixture, use a spice mill or mini-chop or place spices in a plastic bag and smash with the back of a heavy pot. The mixture should not be powdery.
Serve with Fig and Ginger Compote.

1 tbsp coriander seeds	2 tbsp olive oil
1 tsp whole black peppercorns	2 tbsp soy sauce
1 tsp fennel seeds	1 tbsp Dijon mustard
Kosher salt to taste	1 tbsp honey
4 Cornish hens	1 cup chicken stock

Preheat oven to 400 F.

Combine coriander, peppercorns and fennel seeds in small skillet over high heat. Heat spices, shaking pan frequently, for about 1 minute or until fragrant. Remove from heat immediately.

Coarsely crush spices and add salt. Reserve.

Cut down either side of the hen backbones with kitchen shears. Remove wing tips. Turn hens over and remove breastbones. Lay hens flat and coat skin and underside with spice mixture.

Heat oil in skillet on medium-high heat. Cook hens for 2 minutes per side or until golden. Place hens skin side up on rack in roasting pan.

Combine soy sauce, mustard and honey and brush all over hens.

Roast hens for 20 to 30 minutes or until juices are clear. Place hens on carving board.

Skim fat from roasting pan and add stock and any remaining mustard mixture. Bring to boil, scraping up bits on bottom of pan.

Serve hens with sauce.

FIG AND GINGER COMPOTE

In pot, combine 1 lb coarsely chopped figs, 1 cup raisins, 1 tbsp chopped stem ginger in syrup, 1/4 cup granulated sugar, 1/4 cup cider vinegar and 1/4 cup orange marmalade. Stir in 1/2 cup water and 1 cup orange juice. Season with 1 tsp hot red pepper flakes.

Bring to boil, reduce heat and simmer for 25 minutes or until mixture thickens.

Makes 4 to 6 cups.

CHAPTER 6

Meat

When you get to fifty-two, food becomes more important than sex.
– Prue Leith

NEW-STYLE PEPPER STEAK

SERVES 4

Port gives a sweetness to this sauce that balances the spice of the peppercorns. You could substitute Madeira or even use red wine with a tablespoon of sugar.

To crack peppercorns and coriander seeds, place in a plastic bag and bash with a rolling pin or back of a heavy pot.

4 8-oz filet steaks, about 1 1/2 inches thick	1/2 cup Port
2 tbsp olive oil	1 tbsp balsamic vinegar
1 tbsp cracked peppercorns	2 cups beef stock
2 tsp cracked coriander seeds	2 tbsp butter
Kosher salt to taste	• • • • •

Brush steaks with 1 tbsp oil. Coat heavily with peppercorns and coriander seeds. Sprinkle with salt.

Heat remaining 1 tbsp oil in large skillet on high heat. Add steaks and cook for 4 to 5 minutes per side for medium-rare or 6 minutes for medium.

Remove steaks from skillet and keep warm. Discard any fat from skillet. Add Port. Bring to boil on high heat and and reduce until 2 tbsp remains.

Add vinegar and stock to skillet. Bring to boil and cook until reduced to about 1/2 cup. Remove from heat and whisk in butter.

Serve steaks with sauce.

COOKING STEAK

To test whether steaks are ready, use an instant read thermometer — 130 F for rare, 140 F for medium-rare, 150 F for medium. I prefer to stop the cooking when the thermometer reads 5 degrees lower than the recommended temperature because the meat will continue to cook as it rests.

Another test is to watch for the first bubbles of red juice — the sign of a rare steak.

INSTANT BEEF STOCK

Combine a can of beef broth (preferably low salt) with 3 cups water, or use a good-quality commercial stock base and add twice the recommended amount of water. Buy a couple of beef or veal bones from the butcher and simmer stock with bones, a sliced onion, carrot and celery stalk for 1 hour. This will give the stock a gelatinous quality that helps a sauce to thicken when reduced. Sauces made with packaged or canned stocks will not thicken, and they are often too salty.

TUSCAN STEAK

SERVES 2

Rib steaks are a wonderful cut and are especially adaptable to this cooking method where the meat is seared and then roasted for a short time. Serve with crunchy Potato Galette (page 170).

1 tbsp olive oil	1 tbsp lemon juice
1 rib steak on the bone, about 2 inches thick	1/4 cup olive oil
Salt and freshly ground pepper to taste	1/2 bunch arugula
2 tbsp fresh rosemary	1 tbsp balsamic vinegar
1 tbsp grated lemon rind	• • • • •

Preheat oven to 450 F.

Heat oil in ovenproof skillet on high heat. Season steak with salt and pepper and cook for 2 minutes on each side or until browned.

Place skillet in oven and roast steak for 18 to 20 minutes, turning once, until medium-rare. (Bake for 10 minutes longer for medium to well done.)

Place steak on carving board and let rest for 5 minutes.

Combine rosemary, lemon rind and juice and olive oil. Season with salt and pepper.

Divide arugula between 2 plates. Sprinkle with vinegar. Slice steak thinly and fan slices over arugula. Drizzle with rosemary mixture.

PRIME STEAK

Good-quality, well-marbled, aged steaks (such as 1 1/2-inch thick porterhouse) require little enhancement. Brush the meat lightly with olive oil and season with kosher salt and freshly ground pepper. Grill on high heat for about 5 minutes per side for rare or 6 minutes for medium-rare (or use an instant-read thermometer). Let the steaks rest for 2 minutes before carving against the grain into 1/2-inch slices.

Serve with an arugula salad, home fries and some good Dijon mustard.

UP NORTH FLANK STEAK

SERVES 4

This is a cottage classic. It requires little preparation, and it is an inexpensive way to feed a large group (the recipe can easily be doubled). The steak can be either grilled or broiled. Serve with flat beans, sliced tomatoes and a flavored butter (flavored butters freeze well).

1 1/2 lb flank steak	3 tbsp balsamic vinegar
1 tbsp Dijon mustard	3 tbsp olive oil
1 tbsp chopped garlic	Salt and freshly ground pepper to taste

Score flank steak on one side.

Whisk together mustard, garlic, vinegar, olive oil, salt and pepper. Pour over steak and refrigerate for several hours or overnight.

Grill steak for about 3 to 4 minutes per side or until medium rare. Let steak rest on carving board for 5 minutes before slicing against grain.

MUSTARD AND BLACK PEPPER BUTTER

Combine 1/2 cup butter, 2 tsp grainy Dijon mustard and 2 tsp cracked peppercorns in food processor or with hand blender. Season with salt to taste. Place on plastic wrap and roll into log. Refrigerate until needed. Slice thinly and serve with steak.

Makes about 1/2 cup.

HORSERADISH MUSTARD BUTTER

Combine 1/2 cup butter, 1 tbsp Dijon mustard and 1 tbsp grated horseradish in food processor or with hand blender. Place on plastic wrap and roll into log. Refrigerate until needed. Slice thinly and serve with steak.

Makes about 1/2 cup.

CUBAN FLANK STEAK WITH CITRUS MARINADE

SERVES 4

A refreshing way to grill beef. Serve with Chimchurri Sauce and garnish with grilled orange slices.

1 1/2 lb flank steak	1 tsp dried oregano
2 tbsp lime juice	1 tsp paprika
2 tbsp orange juice	1/4 cup olive oil
1 tbsp chopped garlic	Salt and freshly ground pepper to taste
1 tsp ground cumin	• • • • •

Score flank steak on one side.

Combine lime juice, orange juice, garlic, cumin, oregano, paprika and oil. Pour over steak. Marinate for 1 hour at room temperature or refrigerate overnight.

Season flank steak with salt and pepper. Grill for 3 to 4 minutes per side or until medium-rare.

Remove steak from grill and let sit for 5 minutes before slicing against grain.

CHIMCHURRI SAUCE

A typical South American sauce that probably originated in Nicaragua but is now served everywhere. It is particularly popular in Miami, where it is served in upscale Latino restaurants with everything — from a dip with sweet potato fries to a topping for toasted bread. The sauce keeps for two weeks in the refrigerator.

Puree 6 garlic cloves in food processor. Add 2 cups Italian parsley leaves, 1/4 cup lemon juice and 1/2 tsp hot pepper red flakes or to taste. Process until chunky.

With machine running, add 1/2 cup olive oil down feed tube (mixture will thicken).

Makes about 1 cup.

BEEF AND SEAFOOD FONDUE

SERVES 6

This is a beef fondue made without oil. Instead, the beef is simmered in flavored stock. Substitute cubed chicken breast for beef and chicken stock for beef stock, if desired. You could also add scallops or make this dish entirely with seafood, cubing chunks of sea bass, monkfish, salmon or swordfish.

Serve the meat, mushrooms and onions with one or more dipping sauces. When you have finished dipping, pour the stock into soup bowls, garnish with some chopped green onion and serve as a soup to finish the meal.

6 cups beef stock	1 1/2 lb beef tenderloin, cut in 1-inch cubes
6 cloves garlic, peeled	12 shrimp, shelled
1 large onion, sliced	Salt and freshly ground pepper to taste
2 tbsp chopped parsley	12 green onions, white part only
1/4 tsp hot red pepper flakes or to taste	12 oyster mushrooms or shiitake mushrooms, trimmed
Pinch dried thyme	• • • • •

Combine stock, garlic, onion, parsley, hot pepper flakes and thyme in pot. Bring to simmer and simmer for 15 minutes. Strain. (Reserve whole garlic cloves to use in Garlic Aioli).

Pour broth into fondue pot and set over burner.

Season beef and shrimp with salt and pepper.

Spear beef, shrimp, green onions and mushrooms with forks and cook in pot until done to your liking.

HORSERADISH CREAM

Combine 2 tbsp horseradish with 1/2 cup lightly whipped whipping cream or sour cream, salt and pepper.
Makes about 1/3 cup.

GARLIC AIOLI

Puree or mash 6 cooked cloves garlic with 1/2 cup mayonnaise. Season with lemon juice and chopped parsley to taste.
Makes about 1/3 cup.

TOMATO DEVIL SAUCE

Puree 1/2 cup tomato sauce with 1/4 cup salsa, 1 tbsp balsamic vinegar and 1 tsp Worcestershire sauce.
Makes about 3/4 cup.

SHAKING BEEF

This recipe is an adaptation of one of the most popular dishes at the Slanted Door restaurant in San Francisco. It is easy to make at home for a special dinner. Substitute New York sirloin for the tenderloin, if preferred. Serve with Thai jasmine rice and Stir-fried Snow Pea Greens and Mushrooms (page 178).

1 1/2 lb beef tenderloin	SALAD
1 large onion	4 cups baby spinach
1 tbsp chopped garlic	1 cup fresh mint leaves
1 tbsp grated ginger	3 tbsp rice vinegar
1/4 cup soy sauce	1 tbsp soy sauce
2 tbsp oyster sauce	1/4 cup vegetable oil
1 tsp granulated sugar	Salt and freshly ground pepper to taste
2 tbsp cornstarch	Vegetable oil for frying
2 tbsp water	• • • • •
1/2 tsp Asian chili sauce	GARNISH
• • • • •	2 tbsp chopped fresh mint

Cut beef into 3/4-inch cubes. Cut onion in half and slice thinly.

Combine garlic, ginger, 1/4 cup soy sauce, oyster sauce, sugar, cornstarch, water and chili sauce. Toss with beef and marinate for 30 minutes at room temperature or refrigerate for up to 4 hours.

Place spinach and mint on large platter.

Whisk together rice vinegar, 1 tbsp soy sauce and vegetable oil. Toss with salad.

Heat about 1 inch vegetable oil in wok or skillet on high heat. When oil is very hot, add beef cubes in batches along with onions. Cook, tossing occasionally, until beef is rare to medium-rare and onions are browned, about 2 minutes. Remove with a slotted spoon, drain in sieve and place on salad. Repeat with remaining beef. Sprinkle with chopped mint just before serving.

BEEF AND BROCCOLINI STIR-FRY

SERVES 2

A simple stir-fry to serve with blanched broad rice noodles or steamed rice. Broccolini (sometimes called asparation) is a cross between broccoli and kale — sweet but with a slightly bitter edge. Substitute broccoli, asparagus or cauliflower if desired.

8 oz sirloin steak	½ cup chicken stock
2 tbsp white wine	1 tbsp rice vinegar
1 tsp granulated sugar	1 tbsp oyster sauce
1 tbsp soy sauce	2 tsp cornstarch mixed with 1 tbsp water
1 tbsp grated ginger	1 tsp sesame oil
1 tbsp cornstarch	1 green onion, finely chopped
¼ cup vegetable oil	• • • • •
1 bunch broccolini, trimmed and cut in thirds (about 2 cups)	

Trim beef and slice thinly against grain.

Whisk together wine, sugar, soy sauce, ginger and 1 tbsp cornstarch. Add beef and marinate for 30 minutes at room temperature.

Heat oil in wok or skillet on high heat. When oil is very hot, drain meat and add. Do not crowd pan; work in batches, if necessary. Stir-fry meat until cooked on the outside but rare in middle, about 1 minute per batch. Remove meat from wok and reserve. Drain all but 1 tbsp oil from wok.

Add broccolini stems to wok and stir-fry for 1 minute. Add 2 tbsp water, cover and cook for 2 minutes. Add broccolini heads. Cover and steam for 2 minutes.

Stir in stock, vinegar and oyster sauce. Return meat and any juice to wok and combine well.

Add cornstarch mixture, sesame oil and green onion. Bring to boil, stirring until thickened.

GRILLED TURKISH LAMB

SERVES 6

Ask your butcher for a butterflied lamb leg (boned and opened up flat).
Serve this with grilled lemon slices and lots of fresh mint.

1 3-lb boneless leg of lamb, butterflied	½ cup yogurt
1 tbsp chopped garlic	2 tbsp lemon juice
1 tsp harissa (page 6) or Asian chili sauce	3 tbsp olive oil
1 bay leaf, crumbled	Salt and freshly ground pepper to taste
1 tbsp paprika	· · · · ·

Trim fat from lamb. In food processor or by hand combine garlic, harissa, bay leaf, paprika, yogurt, lemon juice, oil, salt and pepper. Spoon marinade on lamb and refrigerate for several hours or overnight.

Place lamb fat side down on grill and sear on high heat for 3 minutes. Turn and sear second side for 3 minutes. Close grill, reduce heat to medium and grill for 10 minutes. Turn again and grill for 10 minutes or until medium-rare.

Remove lamb from grill and let rest for 10 minutes. Carve against grain into thin slices.

LAMB CHOPS WITH SPICED MINT PESTO

SERVES 4

This method of cooking lamb chops leaves them tender and juicy. Serve with Creamy Feta Rice (page 142) and green beans.

¼ cup pine nuts

3 cloves garlic, peeled

1 tsp chopped jalapeño peppers

6 green onions

2 cups fresh mint leaves

½ cup olive oil

3 tbsp lemon juice

Salt and freshly ground pepper to taste

8 loin lamb chops, 1 inch thick

· · · · ·

Combine pine nuts, garlic, jalapeños, green onions and mint leaves in food processor until finely chopped. With machine running, pour oil through feed tube until combined. Add lemon juice, salt and pepper.

Brush some pesto on each lamb chop and place in ovenproof baking dish. Marinate for 1 hour at room temperature.

Preheat oven to 500 F. Bake chops for 3 minutes. Turn off oven and leave chops to cook for 20 minutes.

Serve lamb with remaining mint pesto.

MOROCCAN LAMB BURGERS WITH EGGPLANT JAM

SERVES 4

If you love lamb, this is a wonderful burger, but it is the eggplant mixture that is the real winner. It is very thick and scrumptious.

EGGPLANT JAM	LAMB BURGERS
1 eggplant, peeled and cut in ¹/₂-inch slices	1¹/₂ lb ground lamb
¹/₄ cup olive oil	2 tsp ground ginger
Salt and freshly ground pepper to taste	2 tsp ground cumin
1 tsp chopped garlic	2 tsp paprika
¹/₂ tsp ground cumin	Pinch cayenne
¹/₂ tsp paprika	Salt and freshly ground pepper to taste
¹/₄ tsp cayenne	1 tbsp olive oil
3 fresh or canned tomatoes, chopped	• • • • •
2 tbsp lemon juice or to taste	4 pita breads
2 tbsp chopped parsley	

Brush eggplant on both sides with 2 tbsp oil. Place eggplant on baking sheet.

Broil eggplant for 4 to 5 minutes per side or until browned. Cool and season with salt and pepper. Chop eggplant and reserve.

Heat remaining 2 tbsp oil in skillet on medium heat. Add eggplant, garlic, cumin, paprika and cayenne and sauté until spices are absorbed by eggplant, about 2 minutes. Add tomatoes and stir together.

Reduce heat to low and cook, stirring occasionally, until mixture forms a thick mass, about 20 to 30 minutes. Stir in lemon juice and parsley.

Combine lamb, ginger, cumin, paprika, cayenne, salt and pepper. Form into 4 patties.

Heat oil in skillet or grill pan on medium heat. Add patties and cook for 3 to 4 minutes per side or until medium. Place in pitas and top with eggplant jam.

RACK OF LAMB WITH SPICED ROSEMARY CRUST

SERVES 4

This is an elegant dish for entertaining. Frenching means cleaning the bones so they can be delicately picked up. (The butcher will do this for you.)

¼ cup olive oil

2 lamb racks (8 to 9 chops each), Frenched

Salt and freshly ground pepper to taste

3 tbsp chopped fresh rosemary or 1 tbsp dried

1 tsp chopped garlic

½ tsp chopped jalapeño pepper

or a few drops hot pepper sauce

2 green onions, chopped

⅓ cup fresh breadcrumbs

1 tbsp grainy Dijon mustard

1 tbsp soy sauce

• • • • •

SAUCE

2 tbsp red wine

1 cup beef stock or chicken stock

1 tbsp balsamic vinegar

2 tbsp butter

• • • • •

Preheat oven to 400 F.

Heat 1 tbsp oil in ovenproof skillet on medium-high heat. Place lamb fat side down in skillet and brown on all sides, about 3 minutes per side. Remove from heat, season with salt and pepper and cool.

Combine rosemary, garlic, jalapeño, green onions, remaining 3 tbsp oil, breadcrumbs, mustard and soy sauce in food processor. Combine until paste-like (you could also chop everything finely and combine by hand). Spread breadcrumb mixture all over lamb and return lamb to skillet.

Bake lamb for 25 to 35 minutes or until still pink inside. Remove from skillet and let rest for 10 minutes while finishing sauce. (Any coating that falls into pan should be left there.)

Place skillet on stove on medium heat. Add wine, stock and vinegar. Bring to boil and reduce until ½ cup remains. Remove from heat and whisk in butter.

Carve lamb into chops and drizzle with sauce.

GRILLED PORK CHOPS IN ADOBO

SERVES 4

The secret to grilling pork chops is to use medium-low heat so they remain juicy. Adobo marinade is a fragrant paste of garlic, herbs, cumin and a sour citrus juice that is used extensively in Latin America and Cuba. The sauce goes well with chicken, too.
Serve the pork chops topped with Tomato Ginger Chutney.

1 tsp chopped garlic	1 tsp paprika
1/4 cup lime juice	2 tbsp olive oil
1 tsp ground cumin	Salt and freshly ground pepper to taste
1 tsp chopped fresh oregano or 1/4 tsp dried	4 rib or loin pork chops, 1 inch thick

Combine garlic, lime juice, cumin, oregano, paprika, olive oil, salt and pepper.

Pour over pork chops and marinate for 1 hour at room temperature or refrigerate overnight.

Grill pork chops on medium-low heat for 4 minutes. Turn chops and grill for 4 minutes. Turn and repeat, grilling for 14 to 16 minutes in total, until just cooked.

TOMATO GINGER CHUTNEY

This mouth-watering chutney can accompany any kind of pork, poultry or fish.

Heat 2 tbsp vegetable oil in skillet on medium heat. Add 1 thinly sliced onion and sauté for a few minutes until softened. Stir in 1 tbsp each finely chopped ginger and garlic and cook for about 30 seconds.

Stir in 2 seeded and diced fresh tomatoes and cook until softened. Add 2 tbsp granulated sugar, 2 tbsp white vinegar and 1 tbsp soy sauce. Cook until thickened, about 5 minutes. Add lemon juice and chopped fresh coriander to taste.

Makes about 1 cup.

SWEET POTATO PORK SHEPHERD'S PIE

SERVES 4

A new take on shepherd's pie. Use ground beef or chicken instead of pork, if desired.

1 tbsp vegetable oil	1 bay leaf
1 cup chopped onions	1 cup chicken stock
1/2 cup chopped celery	1 cup chopped canned tomatoes
1/2 cup chopped carrots	2 tsp Worcestershire sauce
1 tsp chopped garlic	• • • • •
1 lb lean ground pork	**SWEET POTATO TOPPING**
Pinch cayenne	3 sweet potatoes, peeled
1 tsp dried savory	1/4 cup butter
1 tsp dried thyme	3 tbsp dry breadcrumbs
Salt and freshly ground pepper to taste	• • • • •

Heat oil in skillet on medium heat. Add onions, celery and carrots and cook until softened, about 3 minutes.

Add garlic, pork, cayenne, savory, thyme, salt and pepper. Sauté for 3 minutes or until pork loses its pinkness. Add bay leaf, stock, tomatoes and Worcestershire. Bring to boil, reduce heat and simmer for 20 to 25 minutes or until sauce thickens.

Cook sweet potatoes in boiling salted water until tender, about 20 to 25 minutes. Drain well and mash with butter. Season with salt and pepper.

Preheat oven to 375 F.

Spoon pork into baking dish. Top with sweet potatoes. Sprinkle breadcrumbs on top.

Bake for 20 to 25 minutes or until topping crisps and mixture bubbles.

PORK TENDERLOIN WITH RHUBARB SAUCE

SERVES 4

In early English cooking rhubarb was an important ingredient in savory sauces because its tart taste balanced the sweetness of the wild game that was commonly served. Today it is making a comeback in sauces.

1 tbsp olive oil	2 cups chopped rhubarb
1/2 tsp dried rosemary	1/2 cup red wine
Salt and freshly ground pepper to taste	1/3 cup granulated sugar
1 1/2 lb pork tenderloin	1/4 cup Dijon mustard

Preheat oven to 400 F.

Combine oil, rosemary, salt and pepper. Rub over pork.

Heat ovenproof skillet on medium heat. Add pork and brown on all sides, about 5 minutes in total.

Transfer skillet to oven and bake for 15 to 20 minutes or until pork is just cooked through.

Remove pork from skillet and keep warm. Add rhubarb, wine, sugar and mustard to skillet. Bring to boil, reduce heat and simmer for 5 to 7 minutes or until thickened.

Slice pork and serve with rhubarb sauce.

SPICY PORK TENDERLOIN WITH TOMATOES

SERVES 2

You can also make this with boneless chicken breasts, but cook for only 15 minutes. Serve with green beans sautéed with coriander.
This recipe can easily be doubled.

2 tsp olive oil	¼ tsp hot red pepper flakes
12 oz pork tenderloin	½ tsp chopped garlic
Salt and freshly ground pepper to taste	1 cup chopped canned tomatoes
1 onion, diced	1 cup chicken stock
1 red pepper, diced	2 small zucchini, diced
1 tbsp chili powder	¼ cup chopped fresh coriander or parsley
1 tsp ground cumin	• • • • •

Heat oil in large skillet on medium-high heat. Season pork with salt and pepper and cook until browned on all sides, about 2 minutes per side. Remove pork and reduce heat to medium.

Add onion and red pepper to skillet and sauté for 2 minutes. Stir in chili powder, cumin, hot pepper flakes and garlic. Cook until vegetables soften, about 2 minutes.

Add tomatoes, stock and zucchini. Bring to boil. Reduce heat to medium-low. Add pork and any juices that have accumulated.

Cover and cook for 20 minutes or until pork is just cooked through. Remove pork and keep warm.

Increase heat to medium-high and cook sauce until slightly thickened. Taste and adjust seasonings if necessary. Stir in coriander.

Slice pork into thin slices and serve with sauce.

TWICE-COOKED GOAT CHEESE
SOUFFLÉS (PAGE 14)

CHILLED PEA SOUP WITH MINT (PAGE 31)

ROASTED SPICY SALMON WITH
MANGO CORIANDER RELISH (PAGE 66)

MUSHROOM RISOTTO (PAGE 145)

MEXICAN CHICKEN WITH GRILLED TOMATO
AVOCADO SALSA (PAGE 86)

HONEY GARLIC SPARERIBS (PAGE 50)

ZESTY BEEF AND MUSHROOM PIE (PAGE 43)

CHOCOLATE TRIFLE (PAGE 196)

YORKSHIRE SAUSAGE JUMBLE

This is best served at brunch or as a light supper dish. Make the sausage mixture and batter ahead of time and combine and bake when needed. If you do not have an ovenproof skillet, cook the sausage mixture in a skillet and then transfer to a baking dish. Heat the dish in the oven for a few minutes and then pour the batter into the hot baking dish.

Use sweet Italian or plain pork sausages. For a vegetarian version, replace the sausages with sautéed mushrooms, onions and spinach, or use leftover roasted vegetables.

1 lb sausages	Salt and freshly ground pepper to taste
1 tbsp olive oil	3 eggs
1 cup sliced onions	$3/4$ cup milk
$1/2$ red pepper, sliced	2 tbsp butter, melted
1 apple, preferably Spy,	$3/4$ cup all-purpose flour
peeled and thinly sliced	• • • • •

Preheat oven to 425 F. Remove sausage meat from casings and crumble.

Heat oil in 8- or 9-inch ovenproof skillet on medium-high heat. Add onions and red pepper to skillet and sauté for about 2 minutes or until vegetables soften. Add sausage meat and sauté for 2 minutes.

Add apple and sauté for 3 minutes or until sausage meat is cooked through. Season with salt and pepper.

Whisk together eggs. Whisk in milk and melted butter. Gradually whisk in flour. Season with salt and pepper.

Pour batter over hot sausage mixture, shaking pan to spread evenly. Bake for 20 to 25 minutes or until puffed and golden. Serve immediately from skillet (it doesn't stay puffed for very long).

SPICY PORK AND BLACK BEANS

SERVES 4

A practically instant chili that can also be made with chicken thighs. Serve with a green salad and buy some cornbread to mop up the juices. Use red or white kidney beans instead of black beans if you wish.

1 tbsp olive oil	1 tsp ground cumin
1 lb pork tenderloin, cut in 1-inch cubes	1 19-oz (540 mL) can black beans, rinsed and drained
1 onion, diced	2 cups chopped canned tomatoes
1 tsp chopped garlic	Salt and freshly ground pepper to taste
1 green pepper, cut in 1-inch pieces	¼ cup chopped fresh coriander or parsley
1 tbsp chili powder	• • • • •

Heat oil in skillet on medium-high heat. Add pork and sauté until browned on all sides, about 6 minutes in total. Remove meat from skillet and reserve.

Add onion, garlic, green pepper, chili powder and cumin to skillet. Sauté until onion softens, about 2 minutes.

Add beans and tomatoes and simmer for 10 minutes. Return pork and any juices to skillet. Cook for 7 to 10 minutes or until pork is no longer pink. Season with salt and pepper and sprinkle with coriander.

PORK SOUVLAKI

SERVES 4

Serve with warm pita bread, a tomato and onion salad and homemade or storebought tzatziki. Use extra bay leaves to thread on skewers, if desired.

1½ lb pork tenderloin, cut in 1½-inch cubes
3 tbsp lemon juice
3 tbsp olive oil
¼ cup white wine

1 tbsp chopped fresh oregano or 1 tsp dried
2 bay leaves, crumbled
Salt and freshly ground pepper to taste
· · · · ·

Toss together pork, lemon juice, oil, wine, oregano and bay leaves. Season well with salt and pepper. Marinate for about 1 hour at room temperature.

Slip pork onto skewers, alternating with bay leaves.

Place on grill on high heat and grill for about 4 minutes per side or until juices run clear.

TZATZIKI

Place 2 cups yogurt in coffee filter and drain for about 1 hour to thicken. Grate 1 English cucumber and sprinkle with salt. Let sit for 30 minutes. Rinse and dry.

Combine drained yogurt, cucumber, 2 tsp chopped garlic, lots of chopped dill, 1 tbsp olive oil and 2 tbsp wine vinegar. Season with salt and freshly ground pepper to taste.

Makes 1½ to 2 cups.

VEAL CHOPS SICILIAN STYLE

SERVES 4

Excellent-quality veal is required for tender and tasty veal chops. Lavender adds scent and flavor to the chops. Use sprigs of fresh lavender as a garnish.

1 tbsp finely chopped dried lavender or rosemary

1 tsp chopped garlic

3 tbsp olive oil

2 tbsp finely chopped Italian parsley

Salt and freshly ground pepper to taste

4 rib veal chops, about 1½ inches thick

½ cup red wine

½ cup chicken stock

¼ cup butter

• • • • •

Combine lavender, garlic, 2 tbsp oil, parsley, salt and pepper. Spread on veal chops. Marinate for 30 minutes at room temperature.

Preheat oven to 425 F.

Heat remaining 1 tbsp oil in ovenproof skillet on medium-high heat. Brown chops for about 2 minutes per side.

Bake chops for 12 minutes or until slightly pink in center. Remove chops from skillet and keep warm.

Add wine to skillet. Bring to boil on high heat and boil until about 2 tbsp remains. Add stock. Boil until reduced by half.

Remove from heat, whisk in butter and spoon sauce over chops.

PROVIMI VEAL

There is no such grade as "provimi" veal. It is the name of a company that produces very fine veal and whose successful PR campaign has made synonymous with good veal. For the finest-quality veal, look for a creamy pink color. Darker veal has more sinew and can be used in slow-cooked dishes such as osso buco.

PROSCIUTTO-WRAPPED VEAL TENDERLOIN

SERVES 6

This special dish was the centerpiece of my last New Year's Eve dinner. Veal can be quite bland, but this recipe injects it with flavor.

Veal tenderloins come in different sizes, so you may need two or three for the full recipe. Marsala is a fortified wine similar to sherry or Port, which could be substituted in this recipe.

8 to 12 thin slices prosciutto	2 tbsp olive oil
24 fresh sage leaves, torn	6 garlic cloves, peeled and sliced
2½ lb veal tenderloin	¼ cup Marsala
2 tsp cracked peppercorns	2 cups chicken stock or veal stock
Salt to taste	2 tbsp butter
2 tsp grated lemon rind	• • • • •

Preheat oven to 400 F.

Lay 4 slices prosciutto overlapping on sheet of parchment or waxed paper. Scatter half the sage leaves over prosciutto. Place tenderloin in middle and season with cracked peppercorns, salt and lemon rind.

Roll prosciutto and sage leaves around tenderloin using paper as a guide. Tie in three places with string. Repeat with other tenderloin(s).

Heat oil in ovenproof skillet over medium-high heat. Add garlic and cook until it begins to turn gold, about 30 seconds. Remove garlic from skillet.

Add veal to skillet. Cook for about 1 minute per side to crisp prosciutto. Drain off any fat and scatter in reserved sliced garlic cloves.

Place skillet in oven and bake for 20 to 25 minutes or until tenderloins are just pink. Remove from skillet to carving board and let rest for 5 minutes.

Add Marsala to skillet on high heat. Bring to boil and boil until Marsala has reduced to 1 tbsp. Add stock and boil for 5 minutes or until beginning to thicken (sauce should lightly coat back of spoon). Reduce heat to low and whisk in butter. Season with salt and pepper if necessary.

Slice tenderloin and serve with sauce.

CHAPTER 7

Noodles, Grains and Rice

Warning: fortune cookies don't care what happens to you.
– Mason Cooley

LINGUINE WILTED SALAD AND PINE NUTS

SERVES 4

A superb first course; serve before Chicken Under a Brick (page 100). Endive and radicchio taste much milder when cooked.

8 oz linguine	1/2 cup crumbled Gorgonzola cheese
1/2 cup olive oil	1/2 cup toasted pine nuts
3 Belgian endives, shredded	2 tbsp red wine vinegar
2 cups shredded radicchio	Salt and freshly ground pepper to taste

Bring large of pot of salted water to boil. Add linguine and boil until al dente, about 12 minutes. Drain, reserving about 1/4 cup pasta cooking water.

Heat oil in large skillet on medium heat. Add endives and radicchio. Cook, stirring, for 3 to 5 minutes or until wilted.

Stir in Gorgonzola, pine nuts and vinegar. Add linguine along with pasta cooking water. Season with salt and pepper. Toss and serve.

BLUE CHEESES

Blue cheeses are among the most intensely flavored available. The cheese is injected with a mold and then pierced to encourage the mold to spread. Stilton is the the most famous English version, Roquefort is the French, and Gorgonzola comes from Italy.

PASTA AL FORNO

SERVES 4

Lasagne and cannelloni are favorites for oven-baked pasta, but any pasta will do. This simple family dish can also be made with storebought ingredients. Buy grilled eggplant and a good tomato sauce and the dish is a snap.

12 oz macaroni, ziti or penne
2 cups tomato sauce
2 tbsp chopped fresh basil
1/4 cup grated Parmesan cheese

Salt and freshly ground pepper to taste
1 eggplant, cut in thin slices and grilled
1 1/2 cups grated mozzarella cheese
· · · · ·

Preheat oven to 400 F.

Bring large pot of salted water to boil. Add pasta and boil until *al dente*, about 12 minutes. Drain.

Combine tomato sauce, basil, Parmesan and cooked pasta. Season well with salt and pepper.

Spread half of pasta evenly over bottom of buttered baking dish. Top with eggplant slices and half of mozzarella. Finish with remaining pasta and mozzarella.

Bake for 15 to 20 minutes or until browned on top and heated through.

GRILLED EGGPLANT

Cut eggplant into slices 1/4 inch thick and brush with olive oil. Grill or broil for about 4 minutes per side or until tender and brown. Cut in strips.

TOMATO SAUCE

Heat 2 tbsp olive oil in pot on medium heat. Sauté 1 chopped onion and 1 tsp chopped garlic until softened. Chop 1 28-oz (798 mL) can tomatoes and stir in along with any juice. Bring to boil and simmer for 25 minutes or until slightly thickened. Season with salt and freshly ground pepper. Add 2 tbsp chopped fresh basil, or 2 tsp dried, just before serving. To make the sauce spicy, add up to 1 tsp hot red pepper flakes.

Makes about 2 cups.

ONE-POT PASTA

SERVES 4

A quick, rich pasta dish for family dinners. Substitute any vegetable you like for the broccoli. Leftover cooked vegetables can be used, too.

12 oz penne

1 head broccoli or broccolini, broken in florets

½ cup whipping cream or milk

½ cup cottage cheese

1 cup diced mozzarella cheese

½ cup grated Parmesan cheese

Pinch hot red pepper flakes

2 tbsp chopped parsley

Salt and freshly ground pepper to taste

• • • • •

Bring large pot of salted water to boil. Add penne and boil for 10 minutes. Add broccoli and cook for 2 minutes or until penne is *al dente* and broccoli is crisp-tender. Drain and return pasta and broccoli to pot.

Add cream, cottage cheese, mozzarella, Parmesan, hot pepper flakes and parsley to pot and stir in. Reduce heat and cook until well combined. Season well with salt and pepper.

PARMESAN CHEESE

There is only one real Parmesan cheese, Parmigiano Reggiano — an aged Italian cow's milk cheese with a rich, nutty flavor. It can be eaten alone as part of a cheese course or used as a grating cheese over pasta.

Grana Padano is also used as a grating cheese. It is less expensive than Reggiano and not aged as long; it has a fresh, sweet taste. North American Parmesan does not have the same flavor as the Italian cheeses.

ORZO AND CAVIAR

SERVES 4

At Toronto Taste, the annual fundraiser for Second Harvest, Massimo Capra from Mistura Restaurant made this decadent orzo dish to showcase the Caviar Centre's finest caviar. You can use smoked salmon instead of caviar in this if you wish.

2 cups orzo	1 cup mascarpone cheese
2 tbsp olive oil	Salt and freshly ground pepper to taste
1 shallot, finely chopped	1/4 cup chopped chives
1/4 cup white wine	Caviar or smoked salmon to taste
1 cup milk	• • • • •

Bring pot of salted water to boil. Add orzo and boil for 10 minutes or until *al dente*. Drain well.

Heat oil in skillet over medium-high heat. Add shallot and cook for 1 to 2 minutes until softened. Pour in wine and cook until wine has almost evaporated, about 2 minutes. Reduce heat to low.

Add milk and whisk in mascarpone. Cook for 2 minutes. Season with salt and pepper and stir in chives and orzo.

Serve topped with caviar or smoked salmon.

SPAGHETTI WITH GRILLED FISH

SERVES 4

My favorite pasta dish is spaghetti with seafood. This is a summer version that includes grilled fish. You can also add shrimp to the mix, if you like. Vary the fish to your taste.

¼ cup olive oil	Salt and freshly ground pepper to taste
1 tsp chopped garlic	2 tbsp chopped fresh oregano or basil
3 cups seeded and chopped	4 jumbo scallops or 8 small ones
fresh or canned tomatoes	8 oz sea bass fillet
½ tsp hot red pepper flakes, optional	8 oz halibut fillet
3 tbsp pesto (page 60)	1 lb linguine

Heat 2 tbsp olive oil in skillet over medium heat. Add garlic and sauté for 1 minute. Add tomatoes and hot pepper flakes. Bring to boil, reduce heat and simmer for 10 minutes or until slightly thickened. Stir in pesto and season with salt and lots of pepper.

Combine remaining 2 tbsp oil and oregano. Brush over scallops and fish and season with salt and pepper.

Bring large pot of salted water to boil. Add linguine and cook until *al dente*, about 10 to 12 minutes. Drain.

Grill fish flesh side down for 3 minutes. Turn and grill skin side down for 4 minutes or until just cooked. Cook scallops for 3 minutes per side for jumbo and 2 minutes for smaller ones.

Remove fish from grill and cut into chunks. Leave scallops whole.

Toss pasta and sauce together. Add any fish juices. Serve pasta in bowls topped with fish and scallops.

FARFALLE WITH PORTUGUESE-STYLE CHICKEN

SERVES 4

Use farfalle or orecchiette in this recipe, as they hold the chicken sauce. The sauce has a Portuguese background and can also be served on buns or over rice, if desired.

12 oz farfalle	1 28-oz (796 mL) can tomatoes,
2 tbsp olive oil	drained and pureed
2 boneless, skinless single chicken breasts,	1 tbsp tomato paste
cut in 1-inch cubes	½ cup thinly sliced hot pickled peppers
Salt and freshly ground pepper to taste	2 tbsp chopped fresh basil
1 tsp chopped garlic	½ cup grated Parmesan cheese
⅓ cup white wine	• • • • •

Bring large pot of salted water to boil. Add farfalle and cook until *al dente*, about 12 minutes. Drain.

Heat oil in large skillet on medium heat. Season chicken breasts with salt and pepper.

Add chicken and garlic to skillet and sauté for 1 minute. Add wine, tomatoes, tomato paste and pickled peppers. Bring to boil, reduce heat and simmer for 5 to 7 minutes or until chicken is no longer pink.

Add cooked pasta to skillet. Toss everything together and sprinkle with basil. Serve with grated Parmesan.

FETTUCCINE WITH TOMATOES, HERBS AND CREAM

SERVES 4

A summery pasta with a strong flavor of fresh herbs. I often use fresh broad Chinese egg noodles to make this dish because they are very light.

2 tbsp butter	4 cups seeded and chopped tomatoes
1 tbsp chopped fresh basil	1/2 cup whipping cream
1 tsp chopped fresh rosemary	Salt and freshly ground pepper to taste
1 tsp chopped fresh sage	12 oz fresh fettuccine
1 tbsp chopped fresh mint	1/2 cup grated Asiago cheese

Heat butter in large skillet on medium-high heat. Add basil, rosemary, sage, mint and tomatoes and cook until tomatoes have formed a sauce, about 5 minutes.

Add cream and bring to boil. Simmer for 2 minutes or until slightly thickened. Season with salt and pepper.

Bring large pot of salted water to boil. Add fettuccine and cook for about 3 minutes.

Drain fettuccine and toss with sauce. Serve with grated Asiago.

ASIAGO CHEESE

Asiago cheese is an Italian partially skimmed cow's milk cheese from the Veneto area. It is is mild and slightly nutty-tasting. It is sold in pieces or small wheels. Asiago grates well and will give pasta dishes a slightly different taste than Parmesan.

ORECCHIETTE WITH TOMATOES, MOZZARELLA AND PROSCIUTTO

SERVES 6 AS AN APPETIZER; 3 AS A MAIN COURSE

This pasta is best served in the summer when cherry tomatoes are at their peak. If you can, use a mixture of red and yellow tomatoes. The pasta is hot and the sauce is cold. For a different presentation, slice the mozzarella and lay in the bottom of individual bowls. Spoon the pasta and prosciutto over the cheese.

1 lb cherry tomatoes, halved or quartered

6 black olives, pitted and sliced

1/4 cup olive oil

2 tsp balsamic vinegar

1/4 cup slivered fresh basil

1 tsp finely chopped garlic

Salt and freshly ground pepper to taste

8 oz orecchiette

4 oz thinly sliced prosciutto, chopped

8 oz buffalo mozzarella or bocconcini, crumbled

1/4 cup shaved Parmesan cheese

• • • • •

Place tomatoes and olives in pasta bowl. Stir in olive oil, vinegar, basil and garlic and allow to sit at room temperature for at least 30 minutes. Season with salt and pepper.

Bring large pot of salted water to boil. Add orecchiette and boil until *al dente*, about 12 minutes. Drain and add to pasta bowl, reserving about **1/4** cup pasta cooking water. Toss with tomato mixture.

Add prosciutto and mozzarella to pasta and combine, adding pasta water as you toss. Sprinkle with Parmesan.

BUFFALO MOZZARELLA

This most prized mozzarella is made from buffalo milk and is sold in balls that have been packed in brine. It is sweeter and has more flavor than regular mozzarella.

LINGUINE WITH ARUGULA AND MUSHROOMS

A quick pasta that can be largely made with ingredients available in the store cupboard.

6 sun-dried tomatoes, soaked and sliced	6 oz shiitake mushrooms,
8 oz linguine	trimmed and sliced
¼ cup olive oil	1 bunch arugula, trimmed and cut in half
2 anchovies, chopped	2 tbsp chopped parsley
1 tsp chopped garlic	Salt to taste
1 tsp hot red pepper flakes	¼ cup grated Parmesan cheese

Cover sun-dried tomatoes with warm water and soak for 15 minutes. Drain and slice tomatoes.

Bring large pot of salted water to boil. Add linguine and cook until *al dente*, about 10 to 12 minutes.

Heat skillet on medium-low heat. Add oil, anchovies, garlic and sun-dried tomatoes and cook gently for 5 minutes or until anchovies have nearly disappeared. Stir in hot pepper flakes.

Increase heat to medium-high. Add mushrooms and sauté until softened, about 4 to 5 minutes. Stir in arugula and parsley.

Drain pasta, reserving ¼ cup pasta water. Toss pasta with sauce. Stir in enough pasta water to thin sauce. Taste for seasoning, adding salt only if needed. Serve with Parmesan.

POPPED RICE NOODLES WITH PORK

SERVES 4

A spectacular dish that kids adore. The popped rice noodles add crunch, and the lettuce and hoisin add a sweet pepperiness. You can use ground turkey or chicken instead of pork, if desired. Serve with Stir-fried Snow Pea Greens (page 178) and rice.

3 tbsp soy sauce	1 tbsp vegetable oil
2 tsp sesame oil	½ cup chopped onions
1 tsp grated ginger	½ cup chopped carrots
8 oz ground pork	½ cup green peas, fresh or defrosted
6 dried Chinese mushrooms	• • • • •
2 cups rice noodles	GARNISH
Vegetable oil for deep-frying	4 cups shredded iceberg lettuce
1 tsp cornstarch	3 tbsp hoisin sauce
1 tbsp water	1 tbsp soy sauce
¼ tsp granulated sugar	2 tbsp rice vinegar
1 tsp rice vinegar	• • • • •

Combine 1 tbsp soy sauce, 1 tsp sesame oil, ginger and pork. Marinate for 30 minutes at room temperature.

Soak mushrooms in ½ cup hot water for 20 minutes. Drain, reserving 2 tbsp liquid.

Break up rice noodles. Heat ¼-inch vegetable oil in skillet on high heat. When very hot, add a handful of rice noodles. As they puff, remove from skillet and pile on plate. Repeat with remaining noodles.

Stir together remaining 2 tbsp soy sauce, remaining 1 tsp sesame oil, reserved mushroom liquid, cornstarch, water, sugar and vinegar.

Heat 1 tbsp vegetable oil in skillet or wok on high heat. Stir in pork, breaking it up as you add it. Stir-fry until it loses its pinkness, about 2 minutes. Add onions, carrots, peas and mushrooms and stir-fry until vegetables soften slightly, about 2 minutes. Stir in soy mixture and bring to boil.

Place shredded lettuce on platter. Combine hoisin, soy sauce and rice vinegar and drizzle over lettuce. Top with noodles and pork.

RICE NOODLES WITH SINGAPORE-STYLE CHICKEN

SERVES 3 OR 4

Food in Malaysia is often the fusion of many Asian styles because of the varied backgrounds of the people, as this dish illustrates.

Serve this as a main course with Stir-fried Baby Bok Choy (page 162). If you don't have rice noodles, you can substitute fresh Chinese egg noodles or cooked spaghettini.

6 oz rice noodles	1 red onion, sliced
12 oz boneless, skinless chicken breasts, cut in 1/2-inch cubes	4 oz green beans, trimmed and cut in 1-inch lengths
Salt and freshly ground pepper to taste	1 cup chicken stock
2 tbsp vegetable oil	3 tbsp soy sauce
1 tbsp grated ginger	2 tbsp lemon juice
1 tbsp chopped garlic	1 tsp granulated sugar
1 tbsp Indian curry paste	2 tbsp chopped fresh coriander

Soak rice noodles in hot water for 20 minutes. Drain well.

Season chicken with salt and pepper.

Heat oil in wok or skillet on high heat. Add ginger, garlic and curry paste. Stir-fry for 30 seconds.

Add chicken to wok and stir-fry until chicken browns slightly, 1 to 2 minutes.

Add onion and green beans to wok and stir-fry for 2 minutes or until vegetables soften. Stir in stock, soy sauce, lemon juice and sugar. Bring to boil, stir in noodles and toss together until noodles are soft, about 2 to 3 minutes. Sprinkle with coriander.

LAOTIAN RICE CASSEROLE WITH CHICKEN

SERVES 4

This is a quick, no-fuss, no-muss dish. It works best using chicken thighs, which have more flavor and texture than chicken breasts, although breasts may be substituted (add them after the rice has steamed for 5 minutes). Use other vegetables as desired. Serve with Asian Slaw (page 93).

6 dried Chinese mushrooms	1½ cups uncooked long-grain rice
1 tbsp vegetable oil	1½ cups chicken stock or water
8 boneless, skinless chicken thighs, cut in 2-inch pieces	2 tbsp soy sauce
	1 tsp Asian chili sauce
½ cup finely chopped onions	½ cup green peas, fresh or defrosted
2 tbsp grated ginger	2 green onions, finely chopped
1 tbsp finely chopped garlic	Salt and freshly ground pepper to taste

Soak mushrooms in ¾ cup hot water for 20 minutes. Drain, reserving liquid, and cut in half.

Heat oil in heavy pot on high heat. Add chicken, onions, ginger and garlic and stir-fry until chicken is lightly colored, about 2 minutes. Remove chicken from pot with slotted spoon.

Add rice, stock, soy sauce, chili sauce and reserved mushroom liquid to pot. Bring to boil and boil for 1 minute.

Reduce heat to low and place chicken and mushrooms over rice. Cover tightly. Cook until rice is just tender and chicken is cooked, about 15 minutes. If rice seems very dry, add ¼ cup water.

Stir in peas and green onions. Cook for 5 minutes longer. Taste and add salt, pepper and extra soy sauce if necessary.

CREAMY FETA RICE

SERVES 2

Cook extra rice when making another recipe and make this yummy rice the next day to serve as a side dish with lamb.

2 tsp olive oil	3 cups cooked rice
1/2 cup chopped red onions	Dash lemon juice
1/2 cup whipping cream	Salt and freshly ground pepper to taste
1/2 cup crumbled feta cheese	· · · · ·

Heat olive oil in skillet over medium heat. Add onions and gently sauté until translucent but not brown, about 2 minutes.

Add whipping cream and feta. Increase heat to high and bring to boil. Boil for 1 minute or until mixture thickens slightly.

Reduce heat to medium, add rice and heat, stirring constantly. Season to taste with lemon juice, salt and pepper.

RICE AND BEANS

SERVES 6

This rustic dish has been recognized as one of the healthiest combinations of protein, fiber and carbohydrate. In Jamaica, pigeon peas are used; in Cuba, black beans. For a quick meal you can use canned beans (rinse and drain and add to the rice along with the water), but cooking your own beans adds flavor and texture. Scotch bonnet peppers are intensely hot. Use milder peppers if desired.

½ cup dried black beans
1 Scotch bonnet chili pepper
1 cup uncooked long-grain rice
1 small onion, chopped
1 tsp finely chopped garlic

¼ cup coconut milk
½ tsp dried thyme
Salt and freshly ground pepper to taste
¼ cup chopped fresh parsley or coriander
• • • • •

Cover beans with water and let soak overnight.

Drain beans and place in pot with whole chili pepper and water to cover. Bring to boil. Reduce heat, cover and simmer for 35 to 45 minutes or until *al dente*.

Drain beans, reserving liquid. Return beans to pot and add 1¼ cups reserved liquid.

Stir in rice, onion, garlic, coconut milk, thyme, salt and pepper. Bring to boil, reduce heat, cover and simmer gently until rice is cooked, about 20 to 25 minutes. Remove chili pepper and taste and adjust seasonings if necessary. Sprinkle with parsley.

QUICK-SOAKING BEANS

Instead of soaking beans overnight, cover with cold water, bring to boil and boil for 2 minutes. Remove from heat, cover and let sit for 1 hour.

QUICK COUSCOUS-STUFFED PEPPERS

SERVES 4

A good vegetarian side dish or main course.

1 cup couscous	1 cup cooked chickpeas
4 red or yellow peppers	¼ cup raisins
2 tbsp olive oil	¼ cup pine nuts
1 cup chopped onions	3 tbsp chopped fresh mint
1 tsp paprika	1 egg, beaten
1 tsp ground ginger	Salt and freshly ground pepper to taste
Pinch cayenne	• • • • •

Preheat oven to 400 F.

Bring 1 cup water to boil and stir in couscous. Remove from heat, cover and let stand for 5 minutes.

Cut tops off peppers and hollow out peppers. Cut small slice from base so peppers can stand upright.

Heat oil in skillet over medium heat. Add onions, paprika, ginger and cayenne and sauté until softened, about 3 minutes. Add chickpeas, raisins and pine nuts and cook for 1 minute. Stir in couscous. Cool for a few minutes, then stir in mint and egg. Season well with salt and pepper.

Stuff couscous mixture into peppers. Replace pepper tops over filling.

Place peppers in oiled baking dish and bake for 20 to 25 minutes or until tender but not collapsing.

MUSHROOM RISOTTO

SERVES 4

Carnaroli is the rice of choice for the best risotto. It is more expensive and harder to find than Arborio, but it is worth seeking out. It has lots of soft starch for a creamy consistency but retains a good firm bite when cooked. Arborio has large plump grains that have a faintly nutty flavor when cooked. It has a slightly stickier texture than Carnaroli.

2 tbsp dried porcini mushrooms	1 cup chopped onions
5 cups hot chicken stock	1/2 tsp chopped garlic
2 tbsp olive oil	1 1/2 cups uncooked Carnaroli or Arborio rice
4 oz oyster mushrooms, trimmed and torn in pieces	2 tbsp butter
	1/2 cup grated Parmesan cheese
4 oz cremini mushrooms, trimmed and sliced	Salt and freshly ground pepper to taste
2 oz shiitake mushrooms, trimmed and sliced	2 tbsp chopped parsley
3 tbsp olive oil	. . . . .

Combine porcini and 1 cup chicken stock. Let sit for 20 minutes. Strain stock back into hot stock and set to simmer gently on stove. Reserve mushrooms.

Heat 2 tbsp olive oil in skillet on medium-high heat. Add fresh mushrooms and reserved porcini. Reserve.

Sauté for about 3 minutes or until tender.

Heat 3 tbsp olive oil in pot over medium heat. Add onions and garlic and sauté for 3 minutes or until onion softens. Stir in rice and cook until rice is coated with oil, about 1 minute.

Pour in about 1 cup hot stock and cook, stirring frequently, until most of liquid is absorbed. Add another 1 cup stock and stir again. Repeat until about 1 cup stock remains, about 15 minutes. Stir in mushrooms and any juices.

Add 1/2 cup stock and cook until stock is absorbed. Rice should be *al dente*. If not, add 1/2 cup more stock.

Beat in butter and Parmesan. Season well with salt and pepper. Sprinkle with parsley.

LENTIL CURRY

SERVES 4

A quick and easy curry that can be served as a side dish or as a vegetarian main course with Curried Green Beans (page 168) and Onion Salad.

2 cups dried red lentils	2 tsp cumin seeds
4 1/2 cups water	1/2 tsp hot red pepper flakes, or to taste
Salt to taste	1 tsp ground turmeric
2 tbsp vegetable oil	2 tbsp chopped fresh coriander

Rinse lentils and place in heavy pot. Cover with water, add salt and bring to boil. Reduce heat to low, cover and cook for 20 to 30 minutes or until tender.

Heat oil in skillet on medium heat. Stir in cumin, hot pepper flakes and turmeric. Cook for about 1 minute or until fragrant. Immediately stir spices into lentils.

Taste and adjust seasonings if necessary. Sprinkle with coriander.

ONION SALAD

In India, this simple salad is served as a condiment.

Thinly slice a large sweet onion. Sprinkle with 2 tbsp lemon juice, salt to taste and garnish with a sprinkling of chopped coriander.

Serves 4.

CHICKPEA, SWISS CHARD AND POTATO CURRY

SERVES 4

Serve this as a vegetarian main course with rice (make a ring of rice and place curry in the center) and condiments such as tomato and onion salad, chutney, raisins and a bowl of grated cucumber mixed with yogurt.

1 bunch Swiss chard	1 lb red potatoes, cut in 1-inch cubes
¼ cup butter	2 cups cooked chickpeas
2 tbsp grated ginger	2 tbsp lemon juice
1 tbsp chopped garlic	Salt and freshly ground pepper to taste
2 tbsp Indian curry paste or 2 tsp curry powder	2 tbsp chopped fresh coriander

Divide chard into leaves and stems. Chop stems into ½-inch pieces. Wash leaves and shred.

Bring large pot of water to boil. Add chard stems and boil for 1 minute. Add leaves and boil for 2 minutes longer. Drain well, pressing lightly to remove as much water as possible. Reserve.

Heat butter in skillet on medium heat. Add ginger, garlic and curry paste. Sauté for 1 minute. Add potatoes and water to cover (about 2 cups). Bring to boil, reduce heat and simmer for 10 minutes or until potatoes are crisp-tender.

Add chard and chickpeas and simmer together for 10 minutes or until all vegetables are cooked.

Season with lemon juice, salt and pepper and sprinkle with coriander.

SCENTED SUNSHINE RICE

Soak 2 cups basmati rice in water for 30 minutes. Drain well. Add to heavy pot along with 2 cups water, 1 tbsp turmeric, 6 whole cloves garlic, 1 tsp cumin seeds and 2 one-inch sticks cinnamon. Bring to boil on high heat.

Cover, reduce heat to low and simmer for 15 to 20 minutes or until rice is tender.

Stir in 2 tsp grated orange rind. Remove cinnamon sticks and season with salt and freshly ground pepper to taste.

Makes 4 cups.

POLENTA

Polenta is cooked cornmeal. Serve as a side dish with Italian dishes or grilled meat or poultry. You can use quick-cooking polenta, which only takes 5 minutes to prepare, but this recipe uses plain cornmeal and is more traditional.

4 cups water or 2 cups water and 2 cups milk

1/2 tsp finely chopped garlic

2 tsp salt

1 cup cornmeal

1/2 cup grated Parmesan cheese

3 tbsp chopped parsley

Freshly ground pepper to taste

· · · · ·

Combine water, garlic and salt in large pot; bring to boil. Add cornmeal in stream, whisking until fully incorporated.

Reduce heat to medium-low and cook, stirring, for 15 minutes or until polenta is thick and slight crust forms on bottom of pot. Stir in Parmesan, parsley and pepper. Taste and add more salt if necessary.

GRILLED POLENTA

Serve with grilled meat or poultry or top with tomato sauce, sautéed mushrooms and cheese for a vegetarian version.

Oil an 8-inch square pan. Spoon in 4 cups cooked polenta and smooth top. Chill for 2 hours or overnight.

Turn polenta out of dish and cut into sections. Brush with oil and grill for 2 to 3 minutes per side.

Serves 4.

BARLEY RISOTTO WITH SPINACH

SERVES 4

Barley has the ability to cook to a creamy consistency similar to Arborio rice, so it makes an excellent, nutty risotto.

5 cups chicken stock or water
2 tbsp olive oil
1 small onion, chopped
1 tsp chopped garlic
1 cup uncooked barley

4 cups baby spinach
Salt and freshly ground pepper to taste
3 tbsp chopped Italian parsley
½ cup grated Parmesan cheese
· · · · ·

Heat stock in pot until simmering.

Heat oil in heavy pot on medium heat. Add onion and cook for 1 minute. Add garlic and sauté for 1 minute or until onion is softened. Stir in barley and cook for 1 minute or until barley is coated with oil.

Add 1 cup hot stock, bring to boil, reduce heat and simmer, stirring occasionally, until barley absorbs most of stock. Add 2 more cups stock, cover and cook for 20 minutes or until most of stock is absorbed.

Stir in 1 cup stock and cook, uncovered, stirring frequently, until stock is absorbed, about 5 minutes. Add remaining stock and spinach and cook and stir until barley is tender, about 15 minutes. If barley seems too dry, add ½ cup extra stock. Season well with salt and pepper.

Beat in parsley and cheese. Serve immediately. (Risotto thickens as it sits but it can be reheated by beating in more stock or water.)

ITALIAN PARSLEY

I always use flat-leafed Italian parsley, which has a slightly different flavor than curly parsley. It is easier to chop and looks better as a garnish.

CHAPTER 8

Vegetables and Side Dishes

I don't like gourmet cooking or "this" cooking or "that" cooking. I like good cooking.
– James Beard

ARUGULA AND POMEGRANATE SALAD

SERVES 4

A colorful salad for fall, when pomegranates are available. If you can't find pomegranate molasses, use honey. Try to buy the more unusual yellow pomegranates — their seeds are much juicier and they do not have crunchy, hard centers.

2 bunches arugula	3 tbsp olive oil
1 pomegranate	Salt and freshly ground pepper to taste
2 tbsp balsamic vinegar	½ cup shaved Parmesan cheese
1 tsp pomegranate molasses or honey	. . . . .

Tear arugula into bite-sized pieces and place in bowl. Cut pomegranate in half and scoop seeds into separate bowl.

Whisk together vinegar, pomegranate molasses and olive oil. Season with salt and pepper.

Toss arugula with dressing and place on 4 plates. Scatter pomegranate seeds over salad. Garnish with shaved Parmesan.

ARUGULA AND RADISH SALAD

Combine 1 bunch arugula and about 8 grated radishes. Whisk together 1 tsp Dijon mustard, 2 tbsp balsamic vinegar and ¼ cup olive oil. Toss salad with dressing and shave Parmesan over top.

Serves 4.

POMEGRANATE MOLASSES

Pomegranate molasses is a thick syrup made from reduced pomegranate juice. It has a sweet-sour taste and is very different from regular molasses. It is a staple in Middle Eastern cooking and can be found at Middle Eastern stores and good gourmet shops. It has also become popular in trendy restaurant kitchens, where it is used in sauces, as a glaze and in marinades for salmon and duck.

ASIAN VEGETABLE AND HERB SALAD

SERVES 4 AS AN APPETIZER; SERVES 6 AS PART OF AN ASIAN MEAL

You can add 4 oz soaked thin rice noodles to the vegetables for a noodle variation. Serve this low-fat salad with Vietnamese Chicken (page 91) or any Asian-flavored grill.

2 tbsp vegetable oil	2 cups watercress, trimmed
2 tsp finely chopped garlic	1/2 cup fresh mint leaves
4 shiitake mushrooms, trimmed and sliced	1/4 cup fresh coriander leaves
1 cup thinly sliced red onions	• • • • •
1/2 red pepper, thinly sliced	DRESSING
8 oz thin asparagus stalks, trimmed and cut in 2-inch lengths	1/4 cup lime juice
1 tbsp soy sauce	2 tbsp Thai fish sauce
Salt and freshly ground pepper to taste	1 tsp grated ginger
2 cups spinach, trimmed	2 tbsp vegetable oil
	1 tsp sesame oil

Heat vegetable oil in skillet on high heat. Add garlic, mushrooms, onions and red pepper. Stir-fry for 1 minute. Add asparagus and stir-fry for 2 minutes. The vegetables should still be crisp.

Stir in soy sauce and season with salt and pepper. Cool.

Combine spinach, watercress, mint and coriander on platter. Scatter vegetable mixture over greens.

Whisk together lime juice, fish sauce, ginger, vegetable oil and sesame oil and toss with salad.

GRILLED ASPARAGUS, AVOCADO AND FENNEL SALAD

SERVES 4 TO 6

Serve this outstanding salad as a first course with grilled garlic-rubbed bread or as a side dish with a simple grilled main course.

1 lb asparagus, trimmed	1 tsp Dijon mustard
2 tbsp olive oil	1 tbsp soy sauce
Salt and freshly ground pepper to taste	2 tbsp rice vinegar
1 small bulb fennel	3 tbsp orange juice
1 avocado	1 tbsp black sesame seeds
· · · · ·	1/3 cup olive oil
ORANGE SOY VINAIGRETTE	Salt and freshly ground pepper to taste
2 tbsp finely chopped shallots or green onions	2 tbsp chopped fresh mint
1 tsp grated ginger	· · · · ·

Brush asparagus with oil and season with salt and pepper. Grill for about 4 to 6 minutes, turning occasionally. Asparagus should be crisp-tender and browned. Remove to platter.

Trim base from fennel bulb and remove core and any stalks. Cut fennel bulb into quarters. With a mandoline or sharp knife, slice very thinly. Add to asparagus.

Cut avocado in half and scoop out flesh with large spoon. Dice and scatter over asparagus and fennel.

Whisk together shallots, ginger, mustard, soy sauce, rice vinegar, orange juice and sesame seeds. Whisk in oil and season with salt and pepper.

Toss salad with dressing. Sprinkle with mint.

CUCUMBER ONION SALAD

SERVES 2; SERVES 3 AS PART OF AN INDIAN MEAL

Similar to a cooling raita, this salad should not be made more than two hours ahead, otherwise the cucumber loses its crunch. Serve with salmon or Indian-inspired dishes.

½ cucumber	2 tbsp lemon juice
½ sweet onion	2 tbsp chopped fresh mint
1 tbsp cumin seeds	Salt and freshly ground pepper to taste
¼ cup yogurt	• • • • •

Dice cucumber and onion and place in bowl.

Heat small skillet on medium heat and add cumin seeds. Cook until seeds become fragrant, about 30 seconds.

Combine cumin, yogurt, lemon juice and mint. Season with salt and pepper and toss with vegetables.

CORIANDER CHUTNEY

Remove stems from 1 large bunch coriander. Place coriander leaves in food processor with 1 tsp chopped hot green chili or ¼ tsp cayenne, 1 tbsp grated ginger, 2 cloves garlic, ½ cup coconut milk or yogurt and 1 tsp garam masala (page 5). Blend until smooth.

Makes about 1 cup.

ENDIVE AND ROASTED ONION SALAD WITH CUMIN VINAIGRETTE

SERVES 4

An unusual mélange of fall vegetables. Serve as an appetizer with toasted baguette slices rubbed with garlic and sprinkled with a little olive oil.

2 red onions, thickly sliced	**CUMIN VINAIGRETTE**
1 tbsp olive oil	1 tsp cumin seeds
4 Belgian endives	3 tbsp balsamic vinegar
1 bunch escarole, frisée or Romaine lettuce,	1 tsp honey
in bite-sized pieces	¼ cup olive oil
· · · · ·	Salt and freshly ground pepper to taste

Preheat oven to 450 F.

Toss onion slices with oil in baking dish and roast for 15 minutes, turning once, until golden and tender.

Cut endives crosswise into ½-inch slices. Place in bowl with lettuce. Top with onions.

Heat skillet on medium heat. Add cumin seeds and toast until just fragrant, about 30 seconds. Remove from skillet immediately.

Whisk together cumin, vinegar, honey and oil. Season with salt and pepper. Toss salad with dressing.

PEAR GINGER FENNEL SALAD

This is a kind of up-market Waldorf salad and makes a good first course.

3 cups diced peeled pears	3 tbsp lemon juice
2 cups diced fennel	¹/₂ tsp cracked fennel seeds
¹/₂ cup chopped pecans	¹/₄ cup finely chopped stem ginger
¹/₂ cup raisins	preserved in syrup
¹/₂ cup mayonnaise	Salt and freshly ground pepper to taste

Combine pears, fennel, pecans and raisins.

Whisk together mayonnaise, lemon juice, fennel seeds and ginger. Season with salt and pepper.

Toss salad with dressing.

BRUSCHETTA SALAD

SERVES 6

Called panzanella in Italian, this salad can be used as a base for grilled fish or chicken, or you can eat it on its own with sliced ham. Make it only when tomatoes are in season.

3 cups cubed day-old Italian bread
2 tbsp red wine vinegar
1/2 tsp Dijon mustard
1 tsp finely chopped garlic
1/2 cup olive oil
4 tomatoes

1 cup diced red onions
3 tbsp chopped Italian parsley
1/2 cup pitted and sliced Kalamata olives
3 tbsp slivered fresh basil
Salt and freshly ground pepper to taste
· · · · ·

Preheat oven to 350 F. Place bread on oiled baking sheet and bake for 10 minutes or until crisp.

Combine vinegar, mustard and garlic. Whisk in oil.

Halve tomatoes and squeeze seeds into bowl. Dice tomatoes, adding any juice to seeds in bowl. Toss bread with tomato juices, seeds and 1/4 cup vinaigrette. Let sit for 30 minutes.

Toss bread lightly with diced tomatoes, onions, parsley, olives and basil.

Stir in remaining vinaigrette and season well with salt and pepper. Serve immediately.

CHERRY TOMATO AND ONION COMPOTE

Cut 8 oz cherry tomatoes in half and combine with 1 cup chopped sweet onion, 2 tbsp chopped fresh basil, 1 tbsp balsamic vinegar and 3 tbsp olive oil. Season with salt and pepper.

Serves 4.

MECHOUIA

SERVES 4

This traditional Tunisian salad is often served topped with quartered hard-boiled eggs and canned tuna for a first course. Serve with couscous or any unsauced fish or chicken dish.

2 large red peppers, halved	1/4 tsp cinnamon
1 fresh red chili or jalapeño pepper, halved	2 tbsp lemon juice
3 plum tomatoes, halved and seeded	2 tbsp olive oil
4 cloves garlic, unpeeled	Salt and freshly ground pepper to taste
2 tsp dried ground coriander	2 tbsp capers
1 tsp caraway seeds	• • • • •

Place peppers, chili and tomatoes cut side down on baking sheet with garlic cloves. Broil until skins of peppers and tomatoes are charred and garlic cloves are softened. Remove vegetables as they are ready. Cool slightly, then skin and seed all vegetables.

Dice peppers and place in bowl.

Puree tomatoes, chili, garlic, coriander, caraway seeds and cinnamon in food processor. Stir in lemon juice and olive oil. Season well with salt and pepper

Toss grilled peppers with tomato dressing. Garnish with capers.

ROASTED POTATO SALAD WITH TOMATOES

SERVES 4

This outstanding salad can be served as a light dinner dish or as part of a summer buffet. Use a soft lettuce such as oak leaf, bibb or Boston.

1 lb small red potatoes, halved

2 tbsp olive oil

Salt and freshly ground pepper to taste

1 cup Herbal Salad Dressing

8 oz green beans, trimmed and cut in half

1/2 cup yellow cherry tomatoes

1/2 cup red cherry tomatoes

1 cup chopped red onions

1/4 cup chopped, pitted black olives

1 head oak leaf lettuce

Chopped chives and tarragon

• • • • •

Preheat oven to 400 F.

Toss potatoes with olive oil, salt and pepper in roasting pan. Roast for 30 to 45 minutes or until tender. Toss with **1/2** cup dressing.

Bring pot of salted water to boil and add green beans. Boil for 4 minutes or until crisp-tender. Refresh with cold water until cool. Drain well and add to potatoes.

Cut tomatoes in half and add to potatoes along with red onions and olives. Season well with salt and pepper and toss with remaining dressing.

Line platter with lettuce. Place salad on top. Garnish with chives and tarragon.

HERBAL SALAD DRESSING

A good dressing for summer salads. Always whisk in the cream at the end to prevent curdling.

Combine 1/4 cup white wine vinegar with 1 tbsp chopped fresh tarragon, 1 tbsp chopped parsley, 1 tbsp chopped chives and 1 tbsp chopped fresh chervil. Whisk in 1/4 cup olive oil and 1/4 cup whipping cream. Season with salt and freshly ground pepper to taste.

Makes about 3/4 cup.

LEEKS VINAIGRETTE

SERVES 4

Use wild leeks in spring if you can find them, but blanch in boiling water for only 1 minute and immediately rinse under cold water until cold.

8 leeks, cleaned (page 38) and cut in half lengthwise, or 4 bunches wild leeks

3 tbsp white wine vinegar

2 tbsp finely chopped parsley

1 tsp Dijon mustard

¹/₄ tsp finely chopped garlic

¹/₂ cup olive oil

Salt and freshly ground pepper to taste

1 head red lettuce

• • • • •

Place leeks in skillet with salted water to cover. Bring to boil. Reduce heat and simmer for 6 to 10 minutes or until crisp-tender. Remove, plunge into cold water and drain well. Dry with paper towels.

Whisk together vinegar, parsley, mustard and garlic. Slowly whisk in oil. Season with salt and pepper.

Pour vinaigrette over leeks and marinate for 30 minutes at room temperature or refrigerate overnight.

Arrange lettuce on individual serving plates and place leeks on top.

WILD LEEKS

Wild leeks are easily recognized by their tulip-like leaves, purplish stems and small onion-like bulb. They are one of the first harbingers of spring — a taste treat. They deliver lots of flavor for such fragile-looking greens, both garlicky and onion-like at the same time. Scrape off the papery outer skin, wash them and trim off the roots (you eat the leaves as well as the bulb). Serve raw in a salad, sauté and serve with pasta or make a pesto using the leeks instead of basil.

STIR-FRIED BABY BOK CHOY

SERVES 4

Baby bok choy is available in Asian markets or specialty food stores. Steam for 2 to 3 minutes and drizzle with soy sauce, or try this stir-fry. If you can't find baby bok choy, use regular bok choy cut in a large dice.

12 oz baby bok choy	1 tbsp oyster sauce
1 tbsp vegetable oil	1 tbsp soy sauce
1 large onion, sliced	Salt and freshly ground pepper to taste
1 tbsp grated ginger	. . . . .

Bring large pot of water to boil. Add bok choy and return to boil. Boil for 1 minute or until slightly softened. Rinse with cold water and drain well.

Heat oil in large skillet or wok on high heat. Add onion and ginger and stir-fry for 1 minute. Add bok choy, oyster sauce and soy sauce and continue to stir-fry until bok choy is heated through, about 2 minutes. Season with salt and pepper.

SHREDDED BRUSSELS SPROUTS WITH PINE NUTS AND PROSCIUTTO

SERVES 4

My family's favourite Brussels sprouts recipe. Because shredded Brussels sprouts don't look like Brussels sprouts, this is a good way to serve them to people who claim to dislike them.

1 lb Brussels sprouts
¼ cup olive oil
4 slices prosciutto, chopped

½ cup pine nuts
Salt and freshly ground pepper to taste
. . . . .

Remove root ends and cores from Brussels sprouts, cut in half and slice thinly.

Heat oil in skillet on medium-high heat. Add prosciutto. Sauté until beginning to crisp, about 1 to 2 minutes. Add sprouts and sauté for 3 minutes. Cover pan and cook for 2 minutes or until sprouts are crisp-tender.

Add pine nuts. Sauté for 1 minute. Season with salt and pepper.

BRAISED BRUSSELS SPROUTS WITH VINEGAR AND DILL

Cut an X in the stalk of each sprout for even cooking; remove any leaves that are brown or soft.

Bring large pot of salted water to boil. Add 1 lb trimmed sprouts. Return to boil and cook for 6 to 8 minutes or until barely tender. Refresh under cold running water and drain well.

Combine sprouts with 1 tbsp cider vinegar, 2 tbsp chopped fresh dill and salt and freshly ground pepper to taste. Place in buttered baking dish and bake, covered, at 375 F for 10 minutes. Uncover and bake for 5 minutes longer.

Serves 4.

CABBAGE WITH SWEET ONIONS AND BALSAMIC

SERVES 4

Cabbage loses a great deal of water in cooking, so what seems like a huge amount becomes manageable. Combine any leftovers with a short pasta and toss with poppy seeds and sour cream.

2 tbsp olive oil	2 tsp granulated sugar
2 cups thinly sliced sweet onions	1 tbsp balsamic vinegar
1 tbsp chopped garlic	Salt and freshly ground pepper to taste
4 cups thinly sliced green cabbage	· · · · ·

Heat oil in large skillet or Dutch oven on medium heat. Add onions and sauté for about 10 minutes or until slightly golden and limp. Add garlic and sauté for 1 minute.

Stir in cabbage and sugar and cook for 20 to 25 minutes, stirring occasionally, until cabbage is well browned. Add vinegar and stir together. Season well with salt and pepper.

SLICING CABBAGE

To slice cabbage, cut into quarters, remove core and slice from the long edge with a sharp chef's knife. You could also use a mandoline, a hand grater/slicer with a sharp blade that allows you to slice things very thinly.

ROASTED CAULIFLOWER

SERVES 4

Roasting cauliflower gives it a sweet flavor without a mushy texture. Cut the cauliflower into small florets.

4 cups cauliflower florets
2 tbsp olive oil

Salt and freshly ground pepper to taste
. . . . .

Preheat oven to 450 F.

Toss cauliflower with oil and season with salt and pepper. Place on baking sheet and roast for 15 minutes or until browned and tender. Turn once during cooking.

ROASTING VEGETABLES

Roasting vegetables brings out their flavor and natural sugars. My favorites are root vegetables such as carrots, parsnips, Jerusalem artichokes, beets, rutabaga and potatoes. Roast root vegetables at 400 F (at 450 F the outside becomes too dark before the inside is tender).

Squash, eggplant, zucchini, mushrooms, tomatoes, asparagus, fennel and peppers are also excellent roasted. Roast them at 450 F.

For crisp, brown roasted vegetables, use a metal pan or baking sheet and heat the the oil in the oven before adding the vegetables.

EGGPLANT GRATIN

SERVES 4

I first tasted this at a restaurant in Provence, where it upstaged the lamb it was served with. Serve with a simple grilled lamb or chicken dish or on its own as a vegetarian main course.
If you can find it, use Sicilian eggplant — a pinkish, football-shaped eggplant with a custard-like texture and very few seeds. It is excellent grilled and baked.

1 large Sicilian eggplant (about 2 lb)	Salt and freshly ground pepper to taste
¼ cup olive oil	1 tbsp all-purpose flour
1 tsp chopped garlic	½ cup milk
1 lb plum tomatoes, seeded and diced	½ cup grated provolone cheese
¼ cup chopped parsley	• • • • •

Preheat oven to 400 F.

Cut eggplant in half. Brush cut sides with 1 tbsp oil and place cut side down on baking sheet. Bake for 40 minutes or until soft. Cool and scoop eggplant from shell. Reduce oven to 375 F.

Heat 3 tbsp oil in skillet on medium-high heat. Add garlic and tomatoes and sauté for 5 minutes or until tomatoes soften. Stir in cooked eggplant and parsley and cook for 5 minutes. Season well with salt and pepper.

Stir in flour and cook for 1 minute. Add milk and bring to boil, stirring. Taste and adjust seasonings if necessary.

Place eggplant mixture in oiled baking dish, top with cheese and bake for 15 to 20 minutes or until cheese browns.

DENGAKU EGGPLANT

SERVES 4

This recipe is based on one of my favorite appetizers at Edo, a Japanese restaurant in Toronto. Serve this succulent, creamy eggplant as a first course or as a side dish with teriyaki chicken or salmon. It also makes a good vegetarian main course served with rice.

Use the long, thin, tender-skinned Japanese or Asian eggplants in this recipe. If they are unavailable, use small regular eggplants.

4 Asian eggplants	2 tbsp rice wine
1/2 cup light miso	4 tsp granulated sugar
1 egg yolk	1/4 cup dashi or chicken stock

Preheat oven to 450 F.

Score skin of eggplants lengthways with several cuts and place on parchment-lined baking sheet. Bake for 20 to 25 minutes or until soft.

Cool eggplants and slice open to expose flesh.

Combine miso, egg yolk, rice wine, sugar and dashi until smooth. Pour evenly over eggplants.

Bake for 5 to 8 minutes or until sauce is glazed. Cut in pieces to serve.

MISO

Miso is a fermented soybean paste made from crushing soybeans with barley or rice. It has a unique, slightly salty taste and is high in protein, amino acids, vitamins and minerals and very low in calories and fat. The Japanese have always regarded miso as a health food and cancer fighter.

Light (yellow or white) miso is sweet and delicate. Try using it in salad dressings instead of oil or as a flavor energizer in soups, sauces or vegetable dishes. The more strongly flavored red or brown miso goes well with hearty soups, beans, vegetables and lentils.

Miso keeps for up to a year in the refrigerator.

MISO GINGER VINAIGRETTE

Toss with cucumber and onion, cooked or raw spinach, steamed broccoli, asparagus or cauliflower.

Whisk 1/4 cup light miso with 1/4 cup rice vinegar, 1 tbsp grated ginger, 1 tsp granulated sugar and 1/2 tsp sesame oil.

Makes about 1/2 cup.

CURRIED GREEN BEANS

SERVES 4

A perfect curry to serve with fish or chicken. Blanched cauliflower or broccoli florets can be used in this recipe, too.

1 tbsp vegetable oil	1 tbsp Thai fish sauce
1 tbsp Indian curry paste	12 oz green beans, trimmed
1 tbsp grated ginger	1 tbsp lemon juice
1 cup coconut milk	2 tbsp chopped fresh coriander or basil

Heat oil in skillet on medium heat. Add curry paste and ginger and stir-fry for 2 minutes. Pour in coconut milk and fish sauce. Bring to boil, reduce heat and simmer for 2 minutes.

Add green beans and simmer for 10 minutes or until beans are cooked but still slightly crunchy. Stir in lemon juice. Garnish with coriander.

THE PERFECT SUMMER BEAN RECIPE

Blanch 12 oz green beans in boiling water for 3 minutes. Drain and rinse with cold water.

Heat 2 tbsp olive oil in skillet on high heat. Add 1 tsp chopped garlic and 3 seeded and chopped plum tomatoes. Sauté until tomatoes soften. Add 1 tbsp chopped fresh oregano and green beans and cook together until beans are hot.

Serves 4.

FENNEL AND POTATO STEW WITH GARLIC

SERVES 4

This delectable dish is wonderful with fish, roast lamb or chicken.

1 lb fingerling or small red potatoes

1 bulb fennel, trimmed

1 head garlic, separated in cloves

3 cups chicken stock

2 tbsp butter

Salt and freshly ground pepper to taste

2 tbsp chopped fennel fronds

. . . . .

Wash potatoes but do not peel. Cut in half lengthwise. Remove core from fennel and cut fennel into 1-inch dice. Peel garlic cloves.

Place potatoes, fennel and garlic in pot. Pour in stock. If stock does not cover potatoes, add water until barely covered. Bring to boil over high heat. Reduce heat and simmer for 15 to 20 minutes or until vegetables are tender.

Remove vegetables from pot. Drain liquid, leaving 2 cups stock in pot. Bring stock to boil on high heat and reduce for about 10 minutes or until about 1/2 cup remains.

Remove stock from heat and whisk in butter. Return vegetables, season well with salt and pepper and simmer on low heat for 5 minutes or until hot. Garnish with fennel fronds.

FINGERLING POTATOES

These are thumb-sized white or red potatoes that do not need to be peeled. They are very good in potato salads, roasted, grilled or sautéed. Some varieties have a mealy, dry texture, while others are moist and creamy. Originally grown in the Andes, they are another trendy "new" heirloom vegetable.

POTATO GALETTE

SERVES 2

Any 6- or 7-inch metal container will work in this dish, but cast iron best holds the heat and results in a beautiful brown base of potatoes. It is important to use clarified butter so the potatoes do not stick to the pan.

¹⁄₃ cup clarified butter, warmed
1 lb Yukon Gold potatoes, peeled and thinly sliced

Salt and freshly ground pepper to taste
· · · · ·

Preheat oven to 425 F.

Spread 3 tbsp butter over bottom of ovenproof skillet. Arrange single layer of potatoes over butter. Season with salt and pepper. Continue layering potatoes, brushing each layer with butter and seasoning it until all potatoes are used up. Top with any remaining butter.

Place skillet on medium heat and cook potatoes until bottom layer starts to brown, about 5 minutes. Cover potatoes with parchment paper and lid or plate that sits right on potatoes. Press down.

Place skillet in oven and bake for 15 minutes. Remove cover and press potatoes down. Bake uncovered for 25 to 30 minutes, pressing down twice more, until potatoes are very tender.

Remove from oven, drain off any excess butter and invert onto serving dish. Cut in half to serve.

CLARIFIED BUTTER

Clarifying butter involves removing the milk solids, leaving behind pure butterfat that does not burn as easily as regular butter. Clarified butter also keeps much longer.

Melt unsalted butter slowly in a small pot. When milk solids rise to the top, remove from heat. Cool slightly and strain through cheesecloth to remove the milk solids.

POTATO PANCAKES

MAKES 8 PANCAKES

For lacy pancakes, sprinkle the potato mixture into the skillet and flatten into loose rounds using the back of a spatula.

3 large Yukon Gold potatoes, peeled (about 1 1/2 lb)

1 egg, beaten

Salt and freshly ground pepper to taste

2 tbsp all-purpose flour

1/4 cup vegetable oil

Grate potatoes in food processor fitted with grating blade. Wrap potatoes in tea towel and wring out excess moisture.

Combine potatoes, egg, salt, pepper and flour.

Heat thin layer of oil in large skillet on medium-low heat. Place 1/4 cup potato mixture in hot oil and flatten with fork into thin round about 5 inches in diameter. Repeat with remaining potatoes (cook in batches, adding oil if necessary). Cook until well browned on both sides and crisp around edges, about 2 to 3 minutes per side. Drain well on paper towels.

CELERY ROOT MASHED POTATOES

SERVES 4

Celery root mashed potatoes go wonderfully with steaks. Substitute fennel if desired. Either way, this is lighter than straight mashed potatoes.

4 Yukon Gold potatoes, peeled and diced

4 cups diced celery root

1/4 cup butter

1/2 cup whipping cream or milk

Salt and freshly ground pepper to taste

. . . . .

Place potatoes and celery root in pot and cover with cold water. Bring to boil and boil for 10 to 15 minutes or until vegetables are tender. Drain well.

Mash with potato masher or electric beaters. Beat in butter and cream. Season well with salt and pepper.

MEDITERRANEAN ROASTED POTATOES

SERVES 4

I prefer to use red potatoes in this recipe, but find that the mini potatoes are too small. Buy larger red potatoes and cut in quarters. The dish will look much better and cook more evenly.

1 lb red potatoes	1 tbsp chopped fresh thyme or 1 tsp dried
1 onion	3 tbsp olive oil
3 plum tomatoes	Salt and freshly ground pepper to taste
1 tbsp chopped fresh rosemary or 1 tsp dried	• • • • •

Preheat oven to 400 F.

Cut potatoes, onion and tomatoes lengthwise into quarters. Seed tomatoes.

Combine potatoes, onion, rosemary, thyme and olive oil in metal baking dish. Season with salt and pepper.

Roast for 30 minutes, add tomatoes, and roast for 30 minutes longer or until potatoes are browned and crisp. Turn occasionally during roasting time.

POTATO GRATIN WITH ONION AND GOAT CHEESE

SERVES 6

A rich potato gratin to serve with roast chicken or lamb for a special dinner.

1/4 cup butter
1 large onion, peeled and thinly sliced
4 oz goat cheese, crumbled
1 cup milk
1 cup whipping cream
2 lb Yukon Gold potatoes, peeled and thinly sliced

1/4 cup chopped fresh herbs (e.g., combination of parsley, sage, chives or rosemary) or 1 tbsp dried
Salt and freshly ground pepper to taste

· · · · ·

Preheat oven to 400 F.

Heat 2 tbsp butter in skillet on medium heat. Add onion and cook, stirring occasionally, until soft and browned, about 10 to 12 minutes.

Heat goat cheese, milk and cream in pot over medium heat, stirring until goat cheese is incorporated.

Layer one-third of potatoes in buttered baking dish. Spread potatoes with half of onions, half of herbs and season with salt and pepper. Drizzle with a little goat cheese mixture. Repeat layers, finishing with layer of potatoes.

Pour remaining hot goat cheese mixture over potatoes. Dot with remaining 2 tbsp butter and bake for 50 to 60 minutes or until potatoes are cooked through and top is browned.

SPINACH AND RAPINI SAG

SERVES 4

A beautiful, simple, emerald-colored dish of greens and mustard seeds with a little added spice. If black mustard seeds are unavailable, use yellow. Serve with fish or poultry.

1 bunch rapini, trimmed	Pinch cayenne
¼ cup butter	2 tsp lime juice
1 tbsp grated ginger	¼ cup yogurt
2 tbsp black mustard seeds	Salt and freshly ground pepper to taste
1 bunch spinach, washed and trimmed	• • • • •

Bring large pot of water to boil. Add rapini and boil for 2 to 3 minutes or until crisp-tender. Refresh with cold water and drain well. Chop finely.

Heat 2 tbsp butter in large skillet over medium-high heat. Add ginger and mustard seeds and stir-fry until fragrant, about 1 minute. Add spinach and stir-fry until spinach is limp, about 1 minute.

Add rapini and cayenne. Cover and steam for 5 minutes. Uncover and reduce heat to low. Stir in lime juice, yogurt and remaining 2 tbsp butter. Season with salt and pepper.

RAPINI WITH GARLIC AND CHILI

SERVES 4

A classic rapini recipe that is excellent with veal or pork. The rapini can also be tossed with cooked pasta and a little pasta-cooking water and topped with grated Parmesan for an easy pasta dish.

1 bunch rapini, trimmed	½ tsp hot red pepper flakes
2 tbsp olive oil	Salt and freshly ground pepper to taste
1 tsp chopped garlic	• • • • •

Bring large pot of salted water to boil. Add rapini, return to boil and boil for 2 to 3 minutes or until rapini is crisp-tender. Drain well.

Heat oil in skillet on medium-high heat. Add garlic, hot pepper flakes and rapini. Toss together for 1 to 2 minutes. Reduce heat, cover and cook for 3 minutes. Season with salt and pepper.

RAPINI

Rapini is another name for broccoli rabe. It is a leafy green with broccoli-like buds. Its slightly bitter, mustardy taste is a perfect foil for rich dishes. For the best texture, always blanch rapini before using.

SQUASH AND ROASTED GARLIC GRATIN

SERVES 6

This is my favorite squash dish. Try serving it with roast turkey or Spiced Cornish Hens (page 105).

1 butternut squash	1/4 cup chopped parsley
2 heads garlic	Salt and freshly ground pepper to taste
2 tbsp olive oil	1/2 cup fresh breadcrumbs
1/4 cup butter	• • • • •

Preheat oven to 400 F.

Cut squash in half and remove seeds. Trim top third from heads of garlic.

Brush cut side of squash and garlic with oil. Place squash cut side down on baking sheet. Wrap garlic in foil.

Bake squash and garlic for 45 minutes or until tender.

Scrape squash flesh into bowl. Squeeze garlic out of heads and add to squash. Beat together with 3 tbsp butter and parsley. Season well with salt and pepper.

Place in buttered baking dish, sprinkle with bread-crumbs, dot with remaining 1 tbsp butter and bake for 20 minutes.

SQUASH ROUNDS

A superb side dish that is both sweet and spicy. Use a couple of Delicata or sweet potato squash (shaped like baking potatoes).

Slice squash into 1/2–inch rounds and gently sauté in 2 tbsp olive oil until golden. Season well with salt and pepper and sprinkle with 1 tbsp grated lemon rind, 1 tsp finely chopped stem ginger preserved in syrup and chopped fresh coriander to taste.

Serves 2 to 4.

STIR-FRIED SNOW PEA GREENS AND MUSHROOMS

SERVES 4

If you cannot find pea greens, usually available in Asian markets, substitute watercress or snow peas.

2 bunches snow pea greens	2 green onions, finely chopped
6 shiitake mushrooms, trimmed	1 tbsp soy sauce
2 tsp vegetable oil	2 tbsp chicken stock or water
1 tsp grated ginger	Salt and freshly ground pepper to taste
1 tsp finely chopped garlic	• • • • •

Trim 1-inch off base of the snow pea green stalks. Slice mushroom caps thinly.

Heat oil in skillet or wok on high heat. Add ginger, garlic and green onions and stir-fry for 30 seconds. Add mushrooms and snow pea greens and stir-fry until mushrooms soften and snow pea greens wilt, about 3 minutes.

Add soy sauce and stock. Bring to boil and season with salt and pepper.

SNOW PEA GREENS

Snow pea greens, or pea shoots, are the tender vines on which snow peas grow. Use young, slender shoots with small leaves. Rinse and stir-fry or serve in salads or as a garnish.

CALABACITAS

SERVES 4 TO 6

This sauté of zucchini and leeks makes a zesty side dish for pork or chicken. Calabacita means squash in Spanish — this is a Mexican inspired dish.

1 tbsp olive oil	2 green zucchini, cut in cubes
1 leek, trimmed and thinly sliced	1 tbsp lemon juice
1 tsp chopped garlic	Salt and freshly ground pepper to taste
1 yellow zucchini, cut in cubes	. . . . .

Heat oil in large skillet on medium heat. Add leek and sauté for 1 minute.

Add garlic and zucchini. Sauté for 5 to 7 minutes or until zucchini is golden and cooked through. Season with lemon juice, salt and pepper.

ZUCCHINI, RED ONION AND TOMATO CONFIT

SERVES 4

A perfect side dish to serve with roast chicken or lamb.

4 zucchini	2 tbsp olive oil
1 red onion	20 basil leaves
20 cherry tomatoes, halved	Salt and freshly ground pepper to taste

Preheat oven to 450 F.

Cut zucchini in half and slice each half into 1-inch semicircles. Cut onion in half and each half into quarters.

Toss zucchini, onion and tomatoes in baking dish with olive oil, basil, salt and pepper. Bake for 20 to 30 minutes or until golden-brown and tender.

SAUTÉED JERUSALEM ARTICHOKES

SERVES 4

Jerusalem artichokes are sometimes called sunchokes. Serve them raw in salads or roast alongside a chicken (they will cook quickly, about 20 to 30 minutes in a 400 F oven). Or try them in this sauté and serve with poultry or fish.

1 lb Jerusalem artichokes	Salt and freshly ground pepper to taste
2 tbsp butter	1 tbsp chopped parsley
1 tbsp vegetable oil	· · · · ·

Scrub or peel artichokes and slice thinly.

Heat butter and oil in skillet on medium heat. Add artichoke slices and sauté for 5 to 10 minutes (cooking time will vary depending on how fresh they are). They are ready when they are still slightly crisp and golden. Season with salt and pepper and sprinkle with parsley.

CHAPTER 9

Desserts

Promises and pie crust are made to be broken.
— Jonathan Swift

ROASTED APPLES WITH APPLE CARAMEL SAUCE

SERVES 4

A mouth-watering recipe for apple- and caramel-lovers. Different apples have different flavors and textures when baked. My favorites are Ida Red or Spy, which are crisp, tart and hold their shape.

4 apples	1 tbsp sherry or Port
1/2 cup raisins	• • • • •
1/4 cup chopped dried apricots	APPLE CARAMEL SAUCE
1/4 cup pecans	2 cups apple juice
1 tbsp brown sugar	3/4 cup brown sugar
1/2 tsp cinnamon	1/2 cup whipping cream

Preheat oven to 400 F.

Peel top third of each apple at stem end. With an apple corer or spoon, core down to blossom of each apple but not all the way through. Cut slice off base so apple doesn't tip.

Combine raisins, apricots, pecans, sugar, cinnamon and sherry in food processor or by hand until finely chopped. Stuff mixture into cored apples and place apples in baking dish.

Combine apple juice and brown sugar in pot and bring to boil. Pour apple juice sauce over apples. Bake for 45 to 50 minutes, basting occasionally, until apples are tender.

Pour dish juices into pot and add cream. Bring to boil and boil until sauce thickens, about 5 to 8 minutes. Pour over apples and serve warm.

APPLE CRANBERRY MAPLE CRISP

SERVES 6

The perfect Canadian fall dessert — superfresh cranberries mixed with new crop apples. Use Spy, Mutsu or Ida Red apples, as they hold their shape and don't fall to mush.

6 apples, peeled, cored and sliced	1/3 cup granulated sugar
1 1/2 cups fresh cranberries	1 cup rolled oats
1 tbsp grated orange rind	1 cup all-purpose flour
2 tbsp orange juice	3/4 cup brown sugar
3 tbsp maple syrup	1/2 cup butter

Preheat oven to 425 F.

Combine apples and cranberries. Stir in orange rind and juice, maple syrup and granulated sugar. Transfer to buttered baking dish.

Combine oats, flour and brown sugar. Cut in butter until mixture resembles coarse breadcrumbs. Sprinkle over fruit.

Bake in lower third of oven for 15 minutes. Reduce heat to 375 F and bake for 30 minutes or until top is golden and juices are bubbling.

UNSALTED BUTTER

Unsalted butter contains less water than salted butter and produces better results when used in cakes, pastries and when finishing sauces.

APRICOT MOUSSE

SERVES 4

A quick dessert that looks beautiful served in glass dishes. Any dried fruit can replace the apricots.

8 oz dried apricots	¹/₄ cup yogurt
¹/₄ cup orange liqueur	2 tbsp honey
¹/₂ cup mascarpone cheese	¹/₄ cup grated bittersweet chocolate

Place apricots and orange liqueur in pot. Cover with water and bring to boil. Set aside and soak for 30 minutes. Pour off any liquid and reserve.

Chop apricots coarsely in food processor. Add mascarpone, yogurt and honey and process until fairly smooth. If mixture is too thick, add some reserved soaking liquid.

Spoon into serving dishes and top with grated chocolate.

MASCARPONE CHEESE

Mascarpone is a triple crème, buttery, high-fat Italian cow's milk cream cheese with a delicate, rich flavor. The best substitute is British clotted cream, although you could use ricotta for a much lighter texture and taste.

GRILLED BANANAS WITH CARAMEL SAUCE

SERVES 4

A quick recipe to serve with ice cream after a family barbecue.

1 cup brown sugar	4 bananas
¼ cup water	1 tbsp lime juice
½ cup whipping cream	• • • • •

Combine brown sugar and water in pot. Bring to boil and boil for 3 minutes. Remove from heat and stir in whipping cream. Return to boil, stirring, reduce heat and simmer for 2 minutes or until slightly thickened.

Peel bananas and brush with lime juice. Grill over high heat for 2 minutes per side or until golden. Serve with warm sauce.

BLUEBERRY AND CREAM UPSIDE-DOWN CAKE

SERVES 8

This incredibly good, unusual berry cake is adapted from an old recipe from the Alsace region of France, where yeast is traditionally used as a leavener in cakes instead of baking powder. The texture of this cake has to be firm in order to stand up to the blueberry juices that streak through it. Serve with lots of crème fraîche or whipped cream.

1 1/3 cups all-purpose flour	3/4 cup granulated sugar
1 tsp rapid-rising dry yeast	1 tsp vanilla
Pinch salt	1/4 cup butter, melted and slightly cooled
1 tbsp grated lemon rind	5 cups fresh blueberries
4 eggs	Sifted icing sugar

Preheat oven to 350 F. Butter 9-inch springform pan and line with parchment paper.

Sift together flour, yeast and salt. Stir in lemon rind.

Beat eggs and 1/2 cup sugar in separate large bowl until thick and glossy and triple in volume. Quickly fold in vanilla and flour/yeast mixture. Fold in melted butter.

Place 3 cups blueberries in bottom of springform pan. Sprinkle with 2 tbsp sugar. Spread with half the batter. Cover with remaining blueberries and sugar, and top with remaining batter.

Bake for 50 to 60 minutes or until cake tester comes out clean. Cool in pan for 10 minutes, then turn out onto plate. Dust with sifted icing sugar.

CRÈME FRAÎCHE

Combine 2 tbsp buttermilk and 1 cup whipping cream in glass jar. Leave on counter in warm place for 24 hours, stirring occasionally, until thickened. Refrigerate for up to 2 weeks.

Makes about 1 cup.

ICED BLUEBERRIES WITH HOT WHITE CHOCOLATE SAUCE

SERVES 4

The burst of frozen berries contrasting with the hot chocolate sauce is a wonderful taste and texture treat. Garnish with fresh lemon balm or mint.

2 cups blueberries
1 tsp grated lemon rind

. . . . .

WHITE CHOCOLATE SAUCE
½ cup whipping cream
4 oz white chocolate, coarsely chopped

Toss berries with lemon rind. Place in metal cake pan. Freeze for 1 to 2 hours or until icy. Place berries in 4 wine glasses.

Bring cream to boil, remove from heat and stir in chocolate until melted. Pour over berries and serve immediately.

WHITE CHOCOLATE

White chocolate is not really chocolate. It is a mixture of sugar, cocoa butter, milk solids and vanilla. Buy a good-quality European product if you can. Avoid white chocolate that lists vegetable shortening as an ingredient.

MOLTEN BROWNIE SOUFFLÉ

SERVES 4 TO 6

A rich, easy chocolate dessert. Serve it warm with the inside moist and runny or cold after the soufflé has firmed up.
Serve with whipped cream.

½ cup butter, diced	1½ cups granulated sugar
2 oz unsweetened chocolate, chopped	Pinch salt
2 oz semisweet chocolate, chopped	1 tsp vanilla
4 eggs, separated	½ cup all-purpose flour

Preheat oven to 350 F.

Line 8-inch square cake pan with parchment paper and butter sides.

Combine butter and all chocolate in pot on low heat. Stir together until chocolate melts. Remove from heat and beat in egg yolks one at a time.

Transfer chocolate mixture to large bowl. Stir in 1¼ cups sugar, salt, vanilla and flour.

Beat egg whites in separate bowl until soft peaks form. Beat in remaining ¼ cup sugar and continue to beat until egg whites are thick and glossy.

Stir one-quarter of beaten egg whites into chocolate mixture. Fold in remaining whites.

Pour batter into cake pan. Place pan in larger roasting pan. Pour boiling water into roasting pan until it comes halfway up sides of cake pan.

Bake for 50 to 60 minutes. Brownies should be crisp on top but fairly runny in center. Cool for 20 minutes before serving.

CASSATA TART

SERVES 6

This splendid no-bake tart takes a few minutes to assemble but tastes as if you spent the whole day in the kitchen. The flavorings can be changed to suit your taste (you can omit the ginger and add nuts, for example).

CRUST
2 cups chocolate cookie crumbs

1/2 cup butter, at room temperature

. . . . .

FILLING
1/2 cup chopped candied
orange rind (page 196)

1/4 cup orange liqueur

2 cups ricotta cheese

1/2 cup granulated sugar

1/4 cup whipping cream

2 tbsp chopped stem ginger in syrup

1/2 cup chopped bittersweet chocolate

. . . . .

TOPPING
3 oz bittersweet chocolate,
coarsely chopped

2 tbsp coffee

1/4 cup butter, at room temperature

. . . . .

Combine cookie crumbs and butter and pat into buttered 8-inch pie plate.

Soak orange rind in liqueur for 30 minutes.

Beat ricotta until smooth. Beat in sugar and whipping cream. Fold in orange rind, liqueur, ginger and chopped chocolate.

Spoon filling into pie shell and smooth top.

Melt chocolate with coffee in pot on low heat. Remove from heat and beat in butter. Cool until slightly thickened but still thin enough to pour. Pour over ricotta. Chill until set, about 2 hours.

CHERRY STRUDEL

SERVES 6 TO 8

Sour cherries are easy to pit — just squeeze out the pits with your fingers. You can also use frozen pitted cherries, but drain them well after defrosting.

FILLING
1 lb sour cherries, pitted
1/2 cup ground almonds
1/2 cup granulated sugar
1/4 cup fresh breadcrumbs
1/4 tsp cinnamon

PASTRY
8 sheets phyllo pastry
1/2 cup butter, melted
1/4 cup granulated sugar
1/4 cup ground almonds

Preheat oven to 375 F.

Combine cherries, almonds, sugar, breadcrumbs and cinnamon for filling.

Lay phyllo on counter and cover with tea towel. Remove one sheet and brush with melted butter.

Combine sugar and almonds and sprinkle about 1 tbsp over butter. Top with second sheet of phyllo. Butter and sprinkle with sugar-almond mixture. Repeat with remaining sheets.

Spread cherry mixture over phyllo about 2 inches from long edge and 1 inch from short edge. Fold in short sides and roll phyllo into strudel shape. Brush with butter and cut 3 slits in top. Place on buttered baking sheet.

Bake for 20 minutes or until top is browned and cherry mixture is bubbling. Serve warm with Schlag.

SCHLAG

This Austrian whipped cream is made by whipping 1 cup whipping cream with 1 tsp cinnamon and 1 tbsp of granulated sugar until soft peaks form.

Makes 2 cups.

BROKEN COOKIE BARS

MAKES 16 BARS

This instant dessert is a Scottish favorite. Place cookies in food processor for a finer crumb or hand-chop them for a coarser look (you need to have some texture). Use any combination of cookies (I like orange-flavored).

8 oz bittersweet chocolate, coarsely chopped

1 cup butter

8 oz broken cookies

1 cup chopped nuts, optional

Melt chocolate and butter in heavy pot over low heat. Remove from heat and stir in cookies and nuts.

Spoon mixture into buttered 8-inch square cake pan. Refrigerate until firm and cut into bars.

GINGERNUT NO-BAKE CHEESECAKE

SERVES 6

This delightful Greek-influenced cheesecake requires no baking and can be put together quickly. If you don't want a ginger crust, substitute graham crackers or chocolate cookies. Use any fruit in season, such as peaches, plums, apricots or cherries. Buy the firm block cream cheese for this recipe rather than the soft variety.

2 cups crumbled ginger snaps
1/2 cup slivered almonds
1/2 cup butter, melted
8 oz cream cheese
1/3 cup yogurt
1/4 cup honey

1 tbsp grated orange rind
· · · · ·
TOPPING
2 cups fresh berries
3 tbsp red currant jelly
· · · · ·

Place ginger snaps and almonds in food processor and process until almonds are finely chopped. Add butter and process briefly.

Butter 9-inch springform pan and line base with parchment paper. Press cookie crumbs into base and 1 to 2 inches up sides. Chill for 30 minutes.

Blend together cream cheese, yogurt, honey and orange rind in food processor until smooth. Spoon into chilled shell. Chill for at least 1 hour.

Arrange fruit on top of cheese. Melt jelly just until liquid and brush over fruit. Remove sides of springform pan before serving.

CHOCOLATE CHERRY SQUARES

SERVES 4

These luscious squares are a wonderful treat at the end of the meal. If you serve them at room temperature they taste like fudge. If you serve them chilled they taste like chocolate truffles.

¹/₄ cup butter, melted	1 cup dried cherries
¹/₃ cup whipping cream	1¹/₄ cups shortbread cookie crumbs
8 oz white chocolate, coarsely chopped	2 oz bittersweet chocolate, melted

Line an 8-inch square pan with plastic wrap.

Bring butter and whipping cream to boil and remove from heat. Stir in white chocolate until melted. Add cherries and cookie crumbs.

Pour mixture into square pan. Chill for at least 2 hours.

Lift plastic wrap out of pan and peel wrap from cookie mixture.

Melt bittersweet chocolate in small pot over low heat and drizzle over cookie mixture. Cut into small squares.

CHOCOLATE TRIFLE

SERVES 8

An elegant dessert that is quick to make and easy to eat. Buy a chocolate cake that can be thinly sliced to make the rounds, or make this as one large trifle.

1 plain chocolate cake
2 oranges, peeled and separated into segments
1/2 cup orange liqueur

1 1/2 cups whipping cream
8 oz white chocolate, coarsely chopped
Candied orange rind

Slice cake 3/4 inch thick and cut out 8 rounds using 3-inch cookie cutter. Fit each round into individual glass bowl.

Place a few orange segments on each piece of cake. Pour 1 tbsp liqueur over each serving and let soak for 1 hour.

Bring cream to boil in small pot. Remove from heat and stir in chocolate. Refrigerate for 3 hours. Remove from refrigerator and whisk until cream holds soft peaks.

Spoon white chocolate whipped cream onto oranges, completely covering them. Garnish with candied orange rind.

CANDIED ORANGE RIND

Combine 1/2 cup water and 1/2 cup granulated sugar in small pot. Boil for 3 minutes or until slightly syrupy. Add slivered rind of 1 orange (do not include white pith) and simmer for 10 to 15 minutes or until translucent. Lift out rind with slotted spoon and dry on parchment paper.

DATE CREAM WITH PISTACHIOS

SERVES 6

Orange flower water is a typical seasoning in Tunisian desserts. There is no real substitute for it so omit if not available. Buy the loose, soft Medjool dates for this recipe.

8 oz Medjool dates, pitted

1 cup ricotta cheese

3 tbsp lemon juice

1/2 tsp vanilla

1/2 tsp cinnamon, or more to taste

1 tbsp orange flower water, optional

1/2 cup whipping cream

1/3 cup chopped pistachio nuts

Combine dates, ricotta, lemon juice, vanilla, cinnamon and orange flower water in food processor. Process until well combined but still a little chunky. Scrape into bowl.

Whip cream until soft peaks form. Fold cream into date mixture. Spoon into glass serving dishes and garnish with pistachios.

FIGS WITH MACADAMIA NUTS

SERVES 4

If figs are unavailable you can use peaches or pears. This is very quick to make and a good finish to a rich meal. Use green or black figs.

12 fresh figs	¼ cup brown sugar
3 tbsp orange juice	½ cup macadamia nuts, cut in half
3 tbsp rum	• • • • •

Preheat broiler.

Cut figs in half and place in buttered baking dish.

Combine orange juice, rum and brown sugar. Spoon over figs. Scatter macadamias between figs.

Broil until beginning to bubble, about 2 minutes. Serve figs with pan juices and nuts.

STRAWBERRY GRATIN

SERVES 4

This dessert is essentially a sabayon poured over fruit. You can make the custard mixture ahead of time, but whisk it occasionally to prevent it from separating. Spread over fruit, then brown lightly. This is attractive served in individual dishes.

4 cups strawberries, hulled	2 eggs
¼ cup orange liqueur	¼ cup granulated sugar
1 egg yolk	. . . . .

Slice strawberries and combine with 2 tbsp orange liqueur in 4 ovenproof dishes.

Preheat broiler.

Combine egg yolk, eggs, sugar and remaining 2 tbsp liqueur in heavy pot. Whisk constantly over medium heat until mixture triples in volume. Pour over berries.

Place under broiler, watching constantly, until lightly browned, about 30 to 60 seconds. Serve immediately.

SABAYON

Sabayon is an egg and wine or liqueur mixture whisked over gentle heat until it thickens. It can be cooled and combined with whipped cream for a cold dessert or served warm on its own or over fruit.

ICE CREAM WITH BLACK PEPPER AND SCOTCH

SERVES 4

Although you might wonder about this dessert, it is weirdly wonderful. (One of my guests swore the pepper was vanilla beans and the sauce was caramel!)
   Do not use a peaty single malt; a mellower blend works better.

2 cups vanilla ice cream	¼ cup Scotch
½ tsp freshly ground pepper or to taste	. . . . .

Scoop ice cream into individual bowls. Sprinkle about 6 grinds black pepper over each portion.

Pour 1 tbsp Scotch over each serving.

FELICIA'S LEMON CAKE

MAKES 1 LOAF

My Scottish cousin makes this incredibly easy, foolproof cake every week. She calls it the one-bowl wonder. I often replace the milk with lemon curd which gives the cake a pound cake-like texture.

1/2 cup butter, at room temperature	Grated rind of 1 lemon
1 cup granulated sugar	2 eggs
1 1/2 cups all-purpose flour	. . . . .
1 1/2 tsp baking powder	GLAZE
1/2 tsp salt	1/2 cup granulated sugar
1/4 cup milk	1/4 cup lemon juice

Preheat oven to 350 F.

Combine butter, sugar, flour, baking powder, salt, milk, lemon rind and eggs in large bowl. Beat with electric mixer until well combined, about 3 minutes.

Place parchment paper on base of loaf pan. Butter sides of pan. Spoon batter into pan.

Bake for 45 to 60 minutes or until cake tester comes out clean. Place on rack. Cool for 10 minutes. Remove from pan, peel off paper and return loaf to pan.

Bring sugar and lemon juice to boil in small pot on high heat. Reduce heat and simmer for 2 minutes or until slightly thickened.

Prick holes in warm cake with a skewer and brush warm syrup over cake. Remove cake from loaf pan.

MANGO HEAVEN

SERVES 4

Serve warm over vanilla ice cream and toasted almonds.

2 tbsp butter	3 tbsp brandy
Grated rind and juice of 1 lime	2 ripe mangoes, peeled and sliced
1 tbsp brown sugar	• • • • •

Melt butter in skillet on medium heat. Add lime rind and juice, sugar and brandy. Stir until sugar dissolves.

Add mangoes and simmer for 2 minutes to heat through.

INSTANT MOCHA MOUSSE

SERVES 4

An instant mousse that keeps for up to three days in the refrigerator. For a stronger coffee taste, use espresso.

3 oz semisweet chocolate, chopped	1 cup whipping cream
¼ cup strong coffee	2 tbsp icing sugar

Combine chocolate and coffee in heavy pot over low heat. Stir until smooth. Remove from heat and pour into cold metal bowl for faster cooling.

Whip cream and icing sugar together until cream is thick and light. Fold into chocolate mixture. Pile into four glass serving dishes and refrigerate until thickened, about 2 hours.

CHOPPING CHOCOLATE

Chop chocolate using a serrated knife. The ridges grip the chocolate and helps it to split apart.

PEAR BISCOTTI

SERVES 4

A palate-pleasing dessert based on the simple but stunning combination of pears and bis-cotti. Serve with whipped cream or ice cream.

5 tbsp butter	2 tsp grated lemon rind
1/2 cup brown sugar	1 tbsp lemon juice
3 large pears, peeled, cored and cut in 8	1 1/2 cups biscotti crumbs (about 3 large)

Preheat oven to 375 F.

Melt 3 tbsp butter in skillet over medium heat. Add sugar and cook for 2 minutes or until slightly foamy.

Add pears, lemon rind and juice. Sauté for 4 to 6 minutes or until pears are tender and sauce reduces slightly.

Combine biscotti crumbs with remaining 2 tbsp butter. Place half the crumbs over bottom of buttered baking dish. Top with all pears and juice. Sprinkle with remaining crumbs.

Bake for 15 to 20 minutes or until golden brown. Serve with whipped cream or ice cream.

PEAR UPSIDE-DOWN TART

SERVES 8

This is a melt-in-your-mouth tart similar to a tarte tatin. It is a staple in my kitchen. Freezing the pastry after it is rolled out seems to make the difference. (The pastry is quite delicate and can be rolled out between two sheets of plastic wrap to prevent breaking.)

PASTRY
1 cup all purpose flour
Pinch salt
1 tbsp granulated sugar
1/2 cup cold butter, cubed
1 tbsp cold water

1 tbsp lemon juice
• • • • •

FILLING
1/4 cup butter, at room temperature
1/2 cup granulated sugar
4 large Bartlett pears, peeled, cored and quartered

Combine flour, salt and sugar in bowl for pastry. Cut in butter until mixture resembles small peas. Stir in water and lemon juice. Turn pastry onto floured board and gently knead together. (Alternatively, make pastry in food processor.)

Roll out pastry to 10-inch round. Place between 2 sheets of plastic wrap and freeze for 1 hour.

Preheat oven to 375 F.

Spread butter in heavy 9-inch ovenproof skillet (do not use non-stick skillet for this, or caramel will separate). Sprinkle with sugar. Lay pears on sugar, round side down, with narrow ends pointing toward center. They should slightly overlap. Fill center with remaining pears.

Place skillet on medium heat and cook for 10 to 15 minutes, shaking pan frequently, until sugar has caramelized. Place skillet on baking sheet.

Remove pastry from freezer and place on top of pears. Trim edges to fit edge of skillet. Place on middle shelf of oven and bake for 35 to 45 minutes or until pastry is golden. (Pastry will shrink down onto pears.)

Remove skillet from oven and place large serving plate on top. Invert tart onto plate. If any pears stick, ease them out and replace. Heat skillet to liquefy any remaining caramel and pour over pears. Serve warm.

FRESH RASPBERRIES AND LAVENDER CREAM

SERVES 4

Use fresh leaves if you have lavender in your garden, and garnish with lavender flowers. If not, substitute dried lavender or use fresh rosemary for a different flavor.

1/4 cup white wine

3 tbsp granulated sugar

2 tbsp chopped fresh lavender leaves or 1 tsp dried

1/2 cup whipping cream

4 cups fresh raspberries

• • • • •

Bring wine, sugar and lavender leaves to boil in small pot on high heat. Reduce heat and simmer for 3 to 5 minutes or until mixture is syrupy. Strain syrup and cool.

Whip cream and lavender syrup together until cream thickens and holds its shape.

Place raspberries in 4 individual serving dishes and top with lavender cream.

HERBS IN DESSERTS

It is fashionable today to add herbs or teas to cookies, custards, crème brûlée and other desserts. Try using rosemary in cookies, thyme with apple mixtures, fennel in cookies and custards, and lavender in anything.

ROASTED RHUBARB MOUSSE

SERVES 4

No more watery rhubarb. Roasting it results in a more concentrated rhubarb flavor and texture as well as a beautiful color. Sweeten to taste after cooking, if desired.

1 1/2 lb fresh rhubarb	1 cup mascarpone cheese
1/3 cup granulated sugar	1/3 cup yogurt

Preheat oven to 350 F.

Cut rhubarb into 1-inch slices. Place in buttered baking dish and sprinkle with sugar. Bake for 20 to 25 minutes or until very soft. Cool.

Combine mascarpone and yogurt in food processor or by hand. Fold in rhubarb and all juices. Chill. Spoon into pretty serving dishes.

Acknowledgements

I am a very fortunate person to be surrounded by so many people who have contributed to my life and to this book.

Thanks to my long-time editor at Random House, Sarah Davies, for acquiring this book and guiding it from inception through to the finished product. Special thanks to Scott Richardson for his artistic direction, which produced such a beautiful book.

Shelley Tanaka is the person who guides me to be a better communicator on the page. Her unerring instinct for what is best never fails.

My associates Eshun Mott, who tested the recipes and suggested new ways at looking at them and Maureen Halushak, who typed, phoned, edited and organized, make my life easier and more pleasurable.

My editors Jody Dunn and Nancy Cardinal at *Food and Drink*, Cecily Ross at the *Globe and Mail* and Marilyn Denis and Chrissy Rejman at *CityLine* all give me the opportunity to express my creativity without putting barriers in my way.

The colour photographs originally appeared in *Food and Drink* and I am most appreciative to the LCBO for letting me use them. Thank you to photographers Colin Faulkner, Rob Fiocca, Chris Freeland, Natalie Kauffman, Per Kristiansen, Vince Noguchi, David Scott and outstanding food stylist Jennifer McLagan.

Andreas Trauttmansdorff photographed the dazzling black and white chapter openers and Natalie Kauffman took the beautiful final shot of the dirty dishes, something all cooks have to live with.

My agent Bruce Westwood, the ultimate foodie, shepherded the book along with advice and good humour.

My growing family is my strength and I appreciate all they do for me — Bruce, Emma, Micah, Katie, Shane, Alex, Natalie, Dad and my brother David and our newest but not final addition Zachary — thank you.

A special thank you to my mother Pearl Geneen whose creativity and passion for food inspires me still and to my nephews Daniel and Julian who show great interest in my food and encourage me to remember that kids have their favourites too.

Lucy Waverman
June 2002